Sew Magical

Paper Piece Fantastical Creatures, Mermaids, Unicorns, Dragons & More

16 Blocks & 7 Projects

Mary Hertel

C&T PUBLISHING

Text copyright © 2020 by Mary Hertel

Photography and artwork copyright © 2020 by C&T Publishing, Inc.

Publisher: Amy Barrett-Daffin

Creative Director: Gailen Runge

Acquisitions Editor: Roxane Cerda

Managing Editor: Liz Aneloski

Editor: Katie Van Amburg

Technical Editor: Linda Johnson

Cover/Book Designer: April Mostek

Production Coordinator: Tim Manibusan

Production Editor: Alice Mace Nakanishi

Illustrators: Linda Johnson and Freesia Pearson Blizard

Photo Assistant: Gregory Ligman

Photography by Estefany Gonzalez of C&T Publishing, Inc., unless otherwise noted

Published by C&T Publishing, Inc., P.O. Box 1456, Lafayette, CA 94549

Library of Congress Cataloging-in-Publication Data

Names: Hertel, Mary, 1955- author.

Title: Sew magical : paper piece fantastical creatures, mermaids, unicorns, dragons & more; 16 blocks & 7 projects / Mary Hertel.

Description: Lafayette, CA : C&T Publishing, 2020.

Identifiers: LCCN 2019056661 | ISBN 9781617459238 (trade paperback) | ISBN 9781617459245 (ebook)

Subjects: LCSH: Patchwork--Patterns. | Appliqué--Patterns. | Fantasy in art. | Animals, Mythical. | Machine sewing.

Classification: LCC TT835 .H44694 2020 | DDC 746.46/041--dc23

LC record available at https://lccn.loc.gov/2019056661

Printed in China

10 9 8 7 6 5 4 3 2 1

Dedication I dedicate this book to my son, Brady, lover of all things mystical and magical. His favorite movies involve fantasy creatures. He is my inspiration and my biggest fan.

Acknowledgments A special thank you to my daughter, Jesi. She is a loyal supporter and my right-hand gal. She accompanies me to my many lectures and vending gigs. I would be lost without her super organizational skills.

Contents

PROJECTS

Introduction

If you love mystical creatures, castles, and knights in shining armor reminiscent of days of old, you will love this book. I have always found fanciful creatures intriguing. This book is filled with patterns of magical mermaids, dragons, unicorns, wizards, and fairies … and so much more! Journey with me through yesteryear into a land of dreams and fairy tales.

Sew Magical is a book of paper-pieced block patterns and several useful projects you can sew them into. This book *does* contain all the steps to learn paper piecing (see Paper-Piecing Basics, next page), but it is different from my previous books in that the patterns are not made for beginners. So if you have never paper pieced before, I recommend practicing your paper-piecing skills using one of my previous books that are great for beginners, such as *Sew Cute & Clever Farm & Forest Friends* (by C&T Publishing; see other titles on page 79), a book with lots of easy blocks. Then progress to these more challenging blocks. If you already are a seasoned paper piecer, prepare yourself for loads of fun!

Another way this book is different: These blocks turn out larger than the blocks in my previous books, which all result in 8″ × 8″ square blocks. In this book, most creatures are a combination of two square blocks 8″ × 8″ sewn together, which result in a rectangular block that is 8″ × 15½″.

And here is something else that *is* the same in all of my books … the block patterns are interchangeable in all of the projects! That means you can conceivably create over 100 different projects from this one book.

I can't wait for you to create these fun and fanciful creatures. With sixteen paper-pieced block patterns and seven projects, this book will help you sew some wonderful creations. If you love to paper piece, this is the book you have been waiting for!

Photo by Gail Cameron

Paper-Piecing Basics

Paper piecing is a simple, straightforward method of sewing a design into a project. Perhaps you have experienced the joy and satisfaction of seeing the finished image after adding the last piece to a jigsaw puzzle. The effects of paper piecing are no different. Anyone with basic sewing skills can master paper piecing, as the approach used in all my previous books (which are tailored for beginners) and this book is essentially sewing by number.

Tools

- Paper (I recommend Carol Doak's Foundation Paper by C&T Publishing.)
- Sharp scissors
- Rotary cutter and mat
- Ruler with an easy-to-read ¼" line (such as Add-A-Quarter ruler by CM Designs)
- Multiuse tool (such as Alex Anderson's 4-in-1 Essential Sewing Tool by C&T Publishing) or seam ripper
- Flat-head straight pins
- Lamp or natural light source
- Sewing machine
- Iron and pressing board

Paper piecing is also a creative means of using up oddly shaped pieces of fabric that might otherwise have been relegated to the scrap pile.

Things to Know

STITCH LENGTH

Set the stitch length at 1.5, which is about 20 stitches per inch. When paper piecing, the stitch perforations must be close together to allow the paper to rip easily, but not so close that ripping out a seam is an impossible task.

PREPARE A CONVENIENT WORK STATION

Have the iron, pressing board, and cutting mat close to the sewing machine. There should be a light source handy for positioning scrap pieces on the back of the block. A window works well during the day and a lamp at night.

THE BUTTERFLY EFFECT

After sewing a seamline, the fabric is flipped behind the numbered piece that you are currently attaching. This creates a butterfly effect, meaning that the fabric scrap needs to be lined up to the seam in such a way that it will cover the space you are sewing after it is flipped into place. If you are concerned that the size of the scrap is insufficient, pin along the seamline and try flipping the scrap into place before sewing the seam. That way, if the scrap does not cover the area sufficiently, you can adjust it or find a larger scrap.

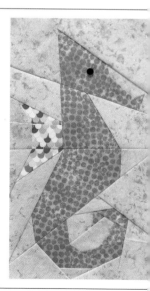

FOLLOW ALONG

If you are new to paper piecing, follow along for practice using the Seahorse block, Part 1 (page 62) and Part 2 (page 63), as you read the following instructions.

Preparing the Patterns

1 Make the recommended number of color copies of the original block. (You need 3 copies for the Seahorse, Part 1 block.)

2 Cut the block into the segments denoted by the capital letters in circles, *adding ¼" seam allowances along the red lines and the outside edges of the block.* For the example, use 1 copy for Segment A, 1 copy for Segments B and D, and 1 copy for Segment C.

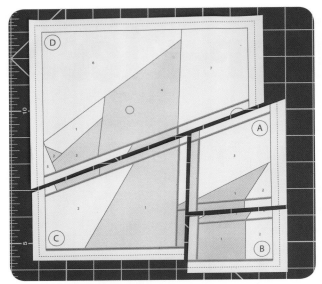

Segments A, B, C, and D with ¼" seam allowances around outside edges

Paper Piecing a Segment

Always stitch pieces in numerical order. Don't forget to set your stitch length (page 7) to 1.5, or about 20 stitches per inch.

1 Pin the *wrong* side of the Piece 1 fabric onto the *unprinted* side of the paper pattern. The right side of the fabric faces you (away from the paper).

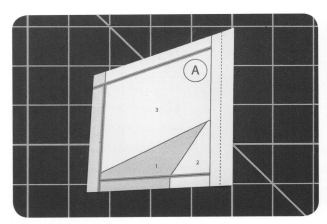

Front side of Segment A

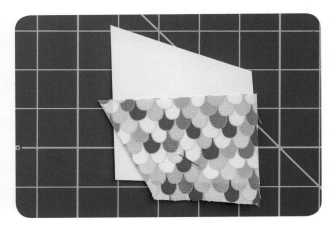

2 Bend the paper pattern and fabric along the seamline between Pieces 1 and 2. Use the side of a pencil, a pressing tool (such as the presser cap on Alex Anderson's 4-in-1 Essential Sewing Tool), or a heavy piece of tagboard (such as a bookmark or postcard) to make the fold. (This will help you align the fabric for Piece 2.)

3 Use the Add-A-Quarter ruler to trim the fabric behind Piece 1 to ¼".

4 Keeping the pattern bent back along the seamline, align the Piece 2 fabric with the fabric from Piece 1. The fabric for Piece 2 will be flipped into place after sewing. Pin in place, right sides together.

Tip: Right Sides Together

As you are piecing, the right sides of fabric should always be together.

---

5 Flip the pattern flat and sew ¼" beyond the seamline at the beginning and the end of this seam (as shown by the green line). No backtacking is needed, as the ends of the seams are stitched over by other seams. Notice that the fabric for Piece 2 is much larger than needed; it will be trimmed later.

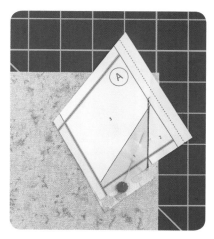

Tip: Double-Check to Avoid Seam Ripping

I like to use large scraps (but no larger than 9″ × 11″) and trim the piece after sewing it in place. As you place the fabric under your presser foot to sew, the seam allowance and the shape you are filling should be to your right. The shape you previously completed should be to your left. Before sewing, do a mental check. Ask yourself these two questions: "Is the piece I am working on to my right?" and "Is the majority of my fabric to my left?" If the answer is yes, then sew. This simple check will eliminate much seam ripping.

6 Flip the fabric into position behind Piece 2 and press. Pin it in place to keep it flat.

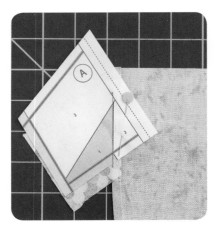

7 Trim the fabric a generous ½″ beyond the first and second edge of Piece 2 (see the dotted lines). *Do not cut the pattern.*

8 Continue to add the remaining pieces in the same manner as you added Piece 2.

Segment A completed

Tip: Stitches Interfering?

Overstitching the seams may at times interfere with an exact fold along a stitching line. In this case, tear the paper just enough to release it from the stitching.

9 Trim the seam allowance of Segment A to an *exact* ¼″ seam, using a rotary cutter, a mat, and a ruler with a ¼″ line.

The segment is now ready to be sewn to the other segments. Follow the same process to make Segments B, C, and D.

Joining Segments

Note: Make sure each segment is trimmed so that it has an exact ¼" seam allowance along the red segment seamline only. Do not trim the outer edge seam allowances at this time.

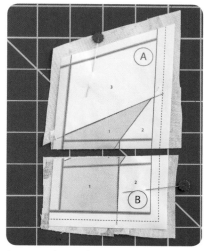

Segments have ¼" seam allowances where they will be joined.

1 With right sides together, pin together the edges of Segments A and B, matching the red sewing lines. Push a straight pin through the end of each red line to help align them as closely as possible. Sew on the red line and ¼" past the red line on both ends.

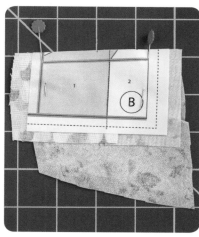

Sew together segments on red line.

2 Remove the paper from the seam allowance to eliminate the possibility of the paper getting trapped under the seams.

3. Press the seam to a side. Let the seam "show" you in which direction it wants to be pressed.

Continue joining segments until Seahorse, Part 1, is complete. Repeat the process of paper-piecing, beginning with Preparing the Patterns (page 8) for Seahorse, Part 2.

Joining Blocks

Blue lines join completed blocks. Unlike red segment seams, blue line seams are backtacked at the beginning and end.

1 Trim only the edges on Part 1 and Part 2 that have a *blue* line. Trim these edges ¼" away from the blue line.

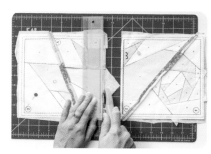

2 Pin the Part 1 and the Part 2 block with right sides together, matching the blue lines.

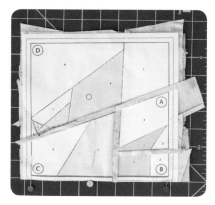

3 Sew on the blue line, backtacking at the beginning and end of the seam. Rip the paper from the seam area. Press the block open.

Tip: Finish Before Trimming

Make sure never to trim the excess fabric from the outer edges of the block until the block is finished and joined to its partner block. After that, it is safe to square up the block using a cutting mat, ruler, and rotary cutter. A rectangular block should measure 8" × 15½" unfinished.

4 Complete any embroidery *while the paper is still attached. The paper acts as a stabilizer and will keep the block from stretching. After the block has been attached to the project, the paper may be removed.* Follow the project instructions to know when buttons and embellishments are added.

Toss Pillow

FINISHED PILLOW: 16½″ × 16½″

This magical pillow will look adorable in any space. The throw pillow is designed for any 8″ × 8″ block—you could even use Part 1 of a rectangular block. It's your choice!

Materials

Refer to your chosen block's materials list for additional paper-piecing and embellishment requirements.

Fabric A: 1 yard for border and pillow back (includes enough for directional fabrics as well)

Fabric B: ⅛ yard *or* 1 fat eighth (9″ × 21″) for inner border

Fabric C: ½ yard for lining (Muslin is recommended.)

Batting: 18″ × 18″ square

Pillow form: 16″ × 16″

Cutting

WOF = width of fabric. Fold fabric selvage to selvage.

Fabric A

• Cut 1 strip 17″ × WOF. Subcut into 2 rectangles 12½″ × 17″ for pillow back and 2 rectangles 4″ × 17″ for outer border.

• Cut 1 strip 4″ × WOF. Subcut into 2 rectangles 4″ × 10″ for outer border.

Fabric B

• Cut 1 strip 1½″ × WOF. Subcut into 2 strips 1½″ × 10″ and 2 strips 1½″ × 8″.

Fabric C

• Cut 1 square 18″ × 18″.

Sewing

Use ¼″ seams throughout, unless otherwise directed.

PAPER-PIECED BLOCK

Refer to Paper-Piecing Basics (page 7) as needed. Refer to Block Patterns (page 44) to choose a block.

1 Paper piece 1 selected square block, using the assorted scraps.

2 Trim the block to 8″ × 8″.

3 Add any necessary embroidery. Do not add any buttons at this time, but mark their placement. If this pillow is to be used for a baby, go ahead and appliqué fabric circles for the eyes instead of using buttons, which might be a choking hazard.

ADD THE INNER BORDER

1 Sew the Fabric B 1½″ × 8″ strips to the top and bottom of the paper-pieced block. Press the seams toward the sashing.

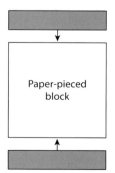

Sew strips to top and bottom of block.

2 Sew the Fabric B 1½″ × 10″ strips to the sides of the paper-pieced block. Press the seams toward the sashing.

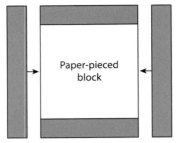

Pillow front should measure 10″ × 10″.

ADD THE OUTER BORDER

1 To add the outer border, follow Add the Inner Border, Steps 1 and 2 (page 13). Use the 2 Fabric A 4″ × 10″ rectangles for top and bottom; then sew the 2 Fabric A 4″ × 17″ rectangles to the sides. Press the seams toward the borders.

2 Remove the paper from the back of the paper-pieced block.

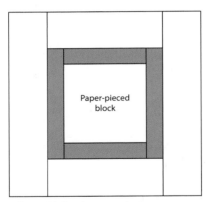

Pillow with borders attached

QUILT THE PILLOW FRONT

1 Layer the pillow lining (right side facing down), batting, and pillow front (right side facing up).

2 Pin together all 3 layers and quilt as desired.

3 Trim the quilted pillow front to 17″ × 17″.

4 Hand sew any required buttons in place.

PREPARE THE PILLOW BACK

1 Hem the Fabric A 12½″ × 17″ rectangles by pressing under 1″ on a 17″ edge of each rectangle. Press under another 1″ on the same 2 edges.

2 Topstitch the pressed edges to form a hem along one edge of each rectangle.

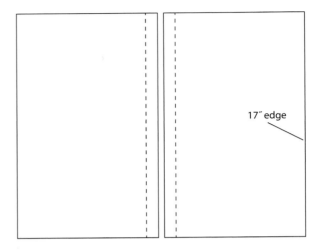

17″ edge

3 With the right sides both facing forward, overlap the hemmed edges of the 2 rectangles by approximately 4″–5″ so the total shape will measure exactly 17″ × 17″. Pin in place.

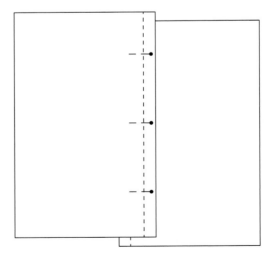

JOIN THE PILLOW FRONT TO THE PILLOW BACK

1 Pin the pillow front to the pillow back, right sides together.

2 Sew around the 4 sides of the pillow, using a ¼″ seam allowance.

3 Remove the pins and turn the pillow right side out. Gently push out the corners. Press the edges flat.

4 Topstitch around the pillow a generous ¼″ from the edge.

5 Slide the 16″ × 16″ pillow form through the back opening.

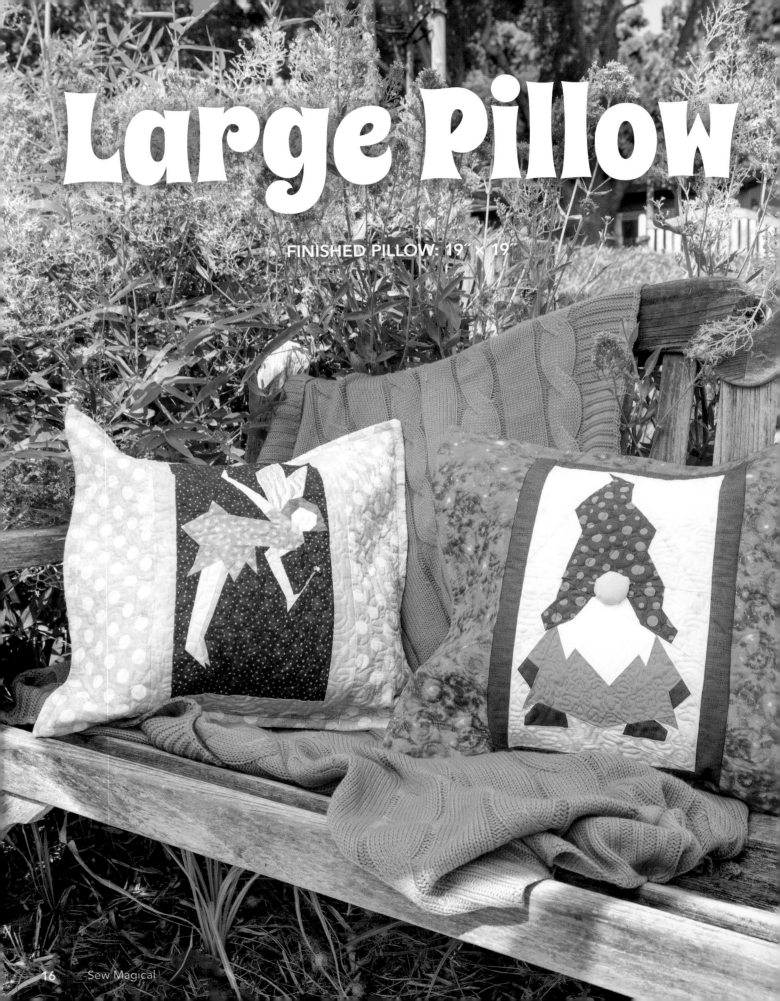

Large Pillow

FINISHED PILLOW: 19˝ × 19˝

This is an adorable pillow to add whimsy to a bed or sofa.

Materials

Refer to your chosen block's materials list for additional paper-piecing and embellishment requirements.

Fabric A: ⅔ yard for main fabric

Fabric B: ⅛ yard *or* 1 fat eighth for inner border

Fabric C: ⅝ yard for lining (Muslin is recommended.)

Batting: 21″ × 21″ square

Pillow form: 18″ × 18″

Cutting

WOF = width of fabric. Fold fabric selvage to selvage.

Fabric A

• Cut 1 strip 13½″ × WOF. Subcut into 2 rectangles 13½″ × 19½″.

• Cut 1 strip 6″ × WOF. Subcut into 2 rectangles 6″ × 21″.

• Cut 1 strip 2″ × WOF. Subcut into 2 strips 2″ × 10″.

Fabric B

• Cut 2 strips 1½″ × WOF. Subcut into 2 strips 1½″ × 17½″ and 2 strips 1½″ × 8″.

Fabric C

• Cut 1 square 21″ × 21″.

Sewing

Use ¼″ seams throughout, unless otherwise directed.

PAPER-PIECED BLOCK

Refer to Paper-Piecing Basics (page 7) as needed. Refer to Block Patterns (page 44) to choose a block.

1 Paper piece 1 selected rectangular block as described in Parts 1 and 2 of your chosen block's instructions.

2 Add any necessary embroidery. Do not add any buttons at this time, but mark their placement. If this pillow is to be used for a baby, go ahead and appliqué fabric circles for the eyes instead of using buttons, which might be a choking hazard.

ADD THE INNER BORDER

1 Sew the Fabric B 1½″ × 8″ strips to the top and bottom of the paper-pieced block. Press the seams toward the sashing.

Sew strips to top and bottom of rectangular block.

2 Sew the Fabric B 1½″ × 17½″ strips to the sides of the block. Press the seams toward the sashing.

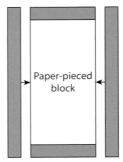

Sew strips to sides of rectangular block.

CONSTRUCT THE PILLOW FRONT

1 Sew the Fabric A 2″ × 10″ strips to the top and bottom of the rectangle. Press the seams toward Fabric A.

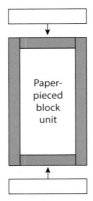

Sew strips to top and bottom of block unit.

2 Sew the Fabric A 6″ × 21″ strips to the sides of the block unit. Press the seams toward Fabric A. *Note: If the strips are longer than necessary, don't worry—the pillow top will be trimmed after quilting.*

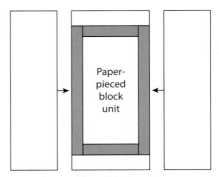

Sew strips to sides of block unit.

QUILT THE PILLOW FRONT

1 Remove the paper from the back of the paper-pieced block.

2 Layer the pillow lining (right side facing down), batting, and pillow front (right side facing up).

3 Pin all 3 layers and quilt as desired.

4 Trim to 19½″ × 19½″, centering the paper-pieced block.

5 Hand sew any required buttons in place.

PREPARE THE PILLOW BACK

1 Hem the Fabric A 13½″ × 19½″ rectangles by pressing under 1″ on a 19½″ edge of each rectangle. Press under another 1″ on the same 2 edges.

2 Topstitch the pressed edges to form a hem along one edge of each rectangle.

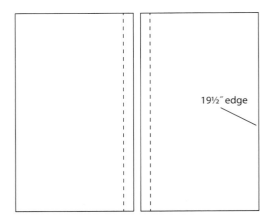

19½″ edge

3 With the right sides both facing forward, overlap the hemmed edges of the 2 rectangles by approximately 4″–5″ so the total shape will measure exactly 19½″ × 19½″. Trim away any excess if necessary.

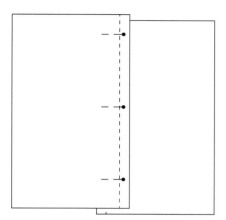

JOIN THE PILLOW FRONT TO THE PILLOW BACK

1 Pin the pillow front to the pillow back, right sides together.

2 Sew around the 4 sides of the pillow, using a ¼″ seam allowance.

3 Remove the pins and turn the pillow right side out. Gently push out the corners. Press the edges flat.

4 Topstitch around the pillow a generous ½″ from the edge.

5 Slide the 18″ × 18″ pillow form through the back opening.

Lap Quilt

FINISHED QUILT: 43½" x 59"

Materials

Refer to your chosen block's materials list for additional paper-piecing and embellishment requirements. All block background fabric amounts are included in this materials list.

Fabric A: 2 yards for background, outer border, and backgrounds of all horizontal paper-pieced blocks

Fabric B: 1 yard for backgrounds of all vertical paper-pieced blocks

Fabric C: 1¼ yards for sashing and binding

Backing: 3 yards

Batting: 52″ × 67″

Cutting

WOF = width of fabric. Fold fabric selvage to selvage.

Fabric A

- Cut 1 strip 8″ × WOF. Subcut into 4 squares 8″ × 8″.
- Cut 5 strips 4½″ × WOF for outer border.
- Cut 1 square 15½″ × 15½″.
- Use remaining fabric to paper piece backgrounds of the 2 horizontal rectangular blocks.

Fabric C

- Cut 6 strips 2½″ × WOF for binding.
- Cut 11 strips 2″ × WOF.

  Subcut 2 strips into 4 rectangles 2″ × 15½″.

  Subcut 1 strip into 4 rectangles 2″ × 8″.

  Use remaining 8 strips for sashing and inner border.

Backing

- Cut 3 yards in half into 2 pieces each 1½ yards long. Sew together the 2 pieces selvage to selvage with a ¾″ seam allowance. Trim off selvages in the seam allowance. Press open.

Sewing

Use ¼″ seams throughout, unless otherwise directed.

PAPER-PIECED BLOCKS

Refer to Paper-Piecing Basics (page 7) as needed. Refer to Block Patterns (page 44) to choose blocks.

1 Paper piece 2 selected horizontal rectangular blocks, using Fabric A as the background fabric and following the instructions for your chosen block.

2 Paper piece 4 selected vertical rectangular blocks, using Fabric B as the background fabric and following the instructions for your chosen block.

3 Paper piece 1 Castle block, using Fabric B as the background fabric and following the instructions for the Castle block (pages 74–78).

4 Add any necessary embroidery. Do not add any buttons at this time, but mark their placement. If this quilt is to be used for a baby, go ahead and appliqué fabric circles for the eyes instead of using buttons, which might be a choking hazard.

CONSTRUCT ROWS 1 AND 3

1 Sew a Fabric C 2″ × 8″ sashing strip to each end of the 2 horizontal paper-pieced blocks. Press the seams toward the sashing.

2 Add a Fabric A 8″ × 8″ square to each sashing strip just added in Step 1. Use all 4 Fabric A squares. Press the seams toward the squares.

CONSTRUCT ROWS 2 AND 4

1 Sew a Fabric C 2″ × 15½″ sashing strip to the right and left sides of the castle.

2 Add a vertical paper-pieced block to each sashing strip just added in Step 1. Press all seams toward the sashing. This creates Row 2.

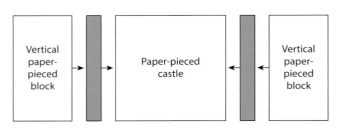

3 Repeat Steps 1 and 2, but this time, use the 15½″ × 15½″ square instead of a Castle block. This creates Row 4.

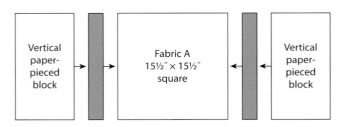

ATTACH THE HORIZONTAL SASHING

1 Sew Fabric C 2″ × WOF strips to the top and bottom of Row 1 and Row 3. Trim all excess sashing.

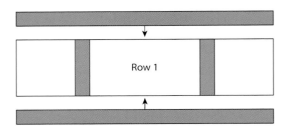

2 Sew Row 2 to the bottom of Row 1.

3 Sew Row 3 to the bottom of Row 2.

4 Sew Row 4 to the bottom of Row 3. Sew a Fabric C 2″ × WOF strip to the bottom of Row 4. Trim the excess. Press all seams toward the sashing.

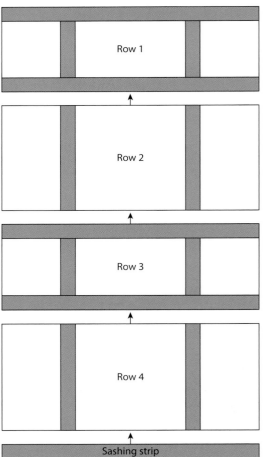

5 Cut 1 Fabric C 2″ × WOF strip in half. This will create 2 short strips 2″ × 21″. Sew one short strip to each of the remaining 2 Fabric C strips to create 2 extra-long sashing strips. Sew these 2 extra-long sashing strips to the sides of the quilt. Press the seams toward the sashing. Trim any excess fabric.

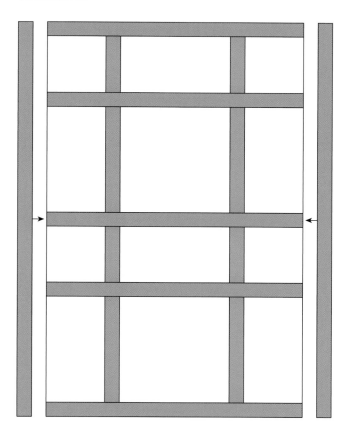

ADD THE BORDERS

1 Sew a Fabric A 4½″ × WOF strip to the top and bottom of the quilt. Trim the excess fabric. Press the seams toward the border.

2 Cut 1 Fabric A 4½″ × WOF strip in half to create 2 rectangles 4½″ × 21″. Sew one of these short strips to each of the remaining 2 Fabric A strips to create 2 extra-long border strips. Sew these 2 extra-long border strips to the sides of the quilt. Trim the excess fabric. Press the seams toward the borders.

QUILTING

1 Remove the paper from the back of the paper-pieced blocks.

2 Layer the backing (right side facing down), batting, and quilt top (right side facing up).

3 Pin together all 3 layers and quilt as desired.

BINDING

1 Pin together 2 Fabric C 2½″ × WOF binding strips, overlapping on a right angle, with right sides together. Mark a diagonal line from Corner A to Corner B.

2 Sew on the diagonal line to connect the strips.

3 Trim the seam to ¼″. Continue, adding the other 4 Fabric C strips in this manner to make 1 long, continuous strip.

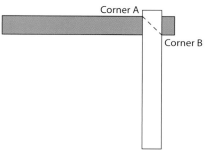

Strips overlap at right angle. Mark and sew on diagonal line.

4 Press the WOF strips in half lengthwise with the wrong sides together.

5 Align the raw edges of the binding strip with the raw edges of the quilt. Bend the beginning of the strip on a right (90°) angle, with the tail facing away from the quilt.

6 Stitch ¼″ from the raw edges. Stop stitching ¼″ from the first corner and backtack.

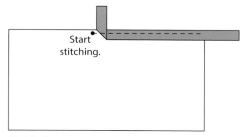

Pin binding strip to quilt and start stitching here.

7 Fold the binding strip straight up. The raw edge of the binding strip should align with the raw edge of the second side of the quilt.

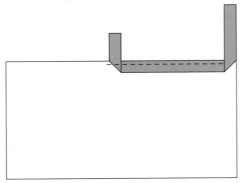

Starting first corner

8 Fold the binding strip straight down to overlap the second edge of the quilt. Start stitching at the top corner and continue until ¼" from the next corner; backtack.

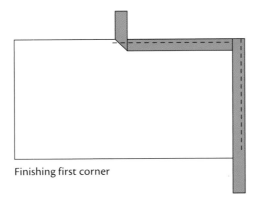

Finishing first corner

9 Continue in this manner around the remaining sides of the quilt, backtacking and turning at each corner.

10 Trim the end of the binding strip so it overlaps the angled beginning section by 2". Trim away the remaining tail.

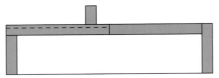

Overlap binding tails.

11 Press the binding around to the back of the quilt and hand stitch in place, easing in the fullness where the tails overlap.

FINISHING

Hand sew any desired buttons on through all thicknesses.

Baby Quilt 1

FINISHED QUILT: 41″ × 41″

Materials

Refer to your chosen block's materials list for additional paper-piecing and embellishment requirements. All block background fabric amounts are included in this materials list.

Fabric A: 1¼ yards for middle border and backgrounds of paper-pieced blocks

Fabric B: ⅝ yard for inner border and binding

Fabric C: 1 charm pack* *or* ⅔ yard fabric for single-fabric outer border

Backing: 2¾ yards

Batting: 49″ × 49″

* *A coordinated collection of (generally 40) precut 5″ squares*

Cutting

WOF = width of fabric. Fold fabric selvage to selvage.

Fabric A

• Cut 1 strip 8″ × WOF. Subcut into 3 squares 8″ × 8″.

• Cut 4 strips 4″ × WOF for middle border.

• Use remaining fabric to paper piece block backgrounds.

Fabric B

• Cut 5 strips 2½″ × WOF for binding.

• Cut 4 strips 1½″ × WOF for inner border.

Fabric C (*from yardage only*)

• *If **not** using a charm pack, cut 4 strips 5″ × WOF.*

Backing

• Cut 2 lengths approximately 49″ × WOF.

Sewing

Use ¼″ seams throughout, unless otherwise directed.

PAPER-PIECED BLOCKS

Refer to Paper-Piecing Basics (page 7) as needed. Refer to Block Patterns (page 44) to choose blocks.

1 Paper piece 3 selected rectangular blocks, using Fabric A for the block backgrounds.

2 Add any necessary embroidery. Do not add any buttons at this time, but mark their placement. If this quilt is to be used for a baby, go ahead and appliqué fabric circles for the eyes instead of using buttons, which might be a choking hazard. If it will be used as a wallhanging, buttons may be used.

CONSTRUCT THE CENTER

1 Sew a Fabric A 8″ × 8″ square to the top of one of the rectangular paper-pieced blocks, and to the bottom of 2 of the blocks. Press the seams toward the square.

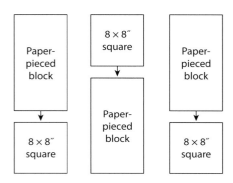

2 Sew together the 3 block units as shown.

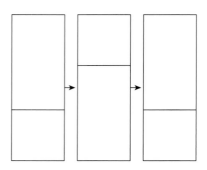

ADD THE INNER BORDERS

1 Sew a Fabric B 1½″ × WOF strip to the top and bottom of the quilt center. Press the seams toward the inner borders. Trim the excess strips.

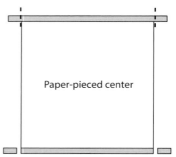

Paper-pieced center

Trim excess inner borders.

2 Repeat Step 1 for the sides of the quilt.

3 Remove the paper from the backs of the blocks.

ADD THE MIDDLE BORDERS

1 Repeat Add the Inner Borders, Steps 1 and 2 (above), but this time use the Fabric A 4″ × WOF strips.

2 Press to the middle borders.

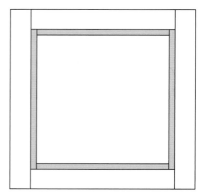

Inner and middle borders attached

ADD THE OUTER BORDER

Option 1: Pieced Border with Charm Squares

1 Sew together 7 charm squares 5″ × 5″ into 1 strip, as shown. Make 2.

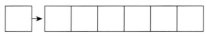

Sew 2 strips of 7 squares each.

2 Sew a pieced border strip to the top and bottom of the quilt. Press the seams toward the middle border.

3 Repeat Steps 1 and 2, this time using 9 charm squares 5″ × 5″ per strip for the quilt's sides.

Sew 2 strips of 9 squares each.

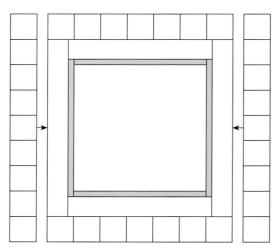

Adding pieced outer borders

4 Press the seams toward the middle borders.

Option 2: Single Fabric Border

Repeat Add the Inner Borders, Steps 1 and 2 (at left), this time using Fabric C 5″ × WOF strips.

QUILTING

1 Sew together the 2 backing pieces along the 49″ edges. Press the seam to one side.

2 Layer the backing (right side facing down), batting, and quilt top (right side facing up).

3 Pin together all 3 layers and quilt as desired.

BINDING

Follow the instructions in Lap Quilt, Binding (page 23), using the Fabric B 2½″ binding strips.

FINISHING

Hand sew any desired buttons on through all thicknesses.

Baby Quilt 2

FINISHED QUILT: 47″ × 30½″

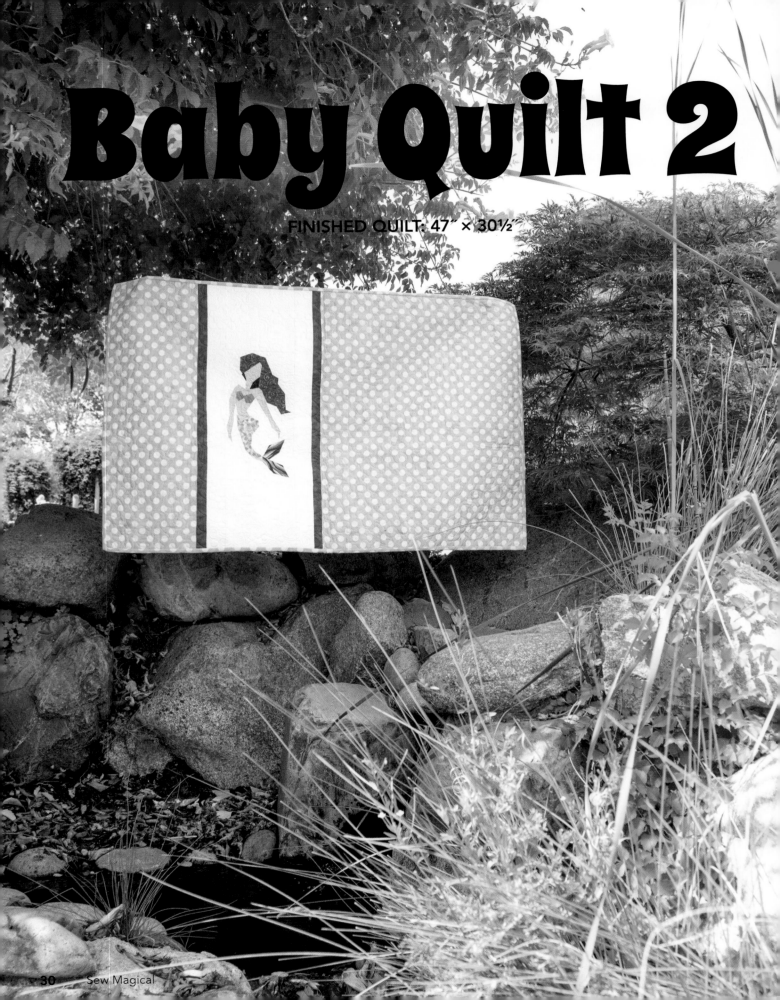

Materials

Refer to your chosen block's materials list for additional paper-piecing and embellishment requirements. All block background fabric amounts are included in this materials list.

Fabric A: ⅔ yard for background of center unit

Fabric B: ⅛ yard for inner border

Fabric C: 1¼ yards for outer sections and binding (nondirectional)

Backing: 1½ yards

Batting: 55″ × 39″

Cutting

WOF = width of fabric. Fold fabric selvage to selvage.

Fabric A

• Cut 1 strip 8″ × WOF. Subcut into 2 squares 8″ × 8″.

• Cut 2 strips 2½″ × WOF.

• Use remaining fabric to paper piece block background.

Fabric B

• Cut 2 strips 1½″ × WOF for inner border.

Fabric C

• Cut 1 strip 30½″ × WOF. Subcut into 1 rectangle 24″ × 30½″ and 1 rectangle 10″ × 30½″.

• Cut 5 strips 2½″ × WOF for binding.

Sewing

Use ¼″ seams throughout, unless otherwise directed.

PAPER-PIECED BLOCK

Refer to Paper-Piecing Basics (page 7) as needed. Refer to Block Patterns (page 44) to choose a block.

1 Paper piece 1 selected rectangular block, using Fabric A for the background.

2 Add any necessary embroidery. Do not add any buttons at this time, but mark their placement. If this quilt is to be used for a baby, go ahead and appliqué fabric circles for the eyes instead of using buttons, which might be a choking hazard. If it will be used as a wallhanging, buttons may be used.

CONSTRUCT THE CENTER UNIT

1 Sew a Fabric A 8″ × 8″ square to the top and bottom of the paper-pieced block. Press the seams toward the squares.

2 Sew a Fabric A 2½″ × WOF strip to each side of the paper-pieced unit. Press the seams toward the strips.

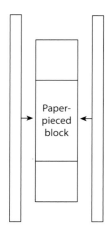

3 Trim the excess fabric from the strips using a ruler and rotary cutter.

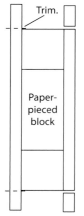

Trim excess fabric.

4 Remove the paper from the back of the paper-pieced block.

ADD THE INNER BORDERS

1 Sew a Fabric B 1½″ × WOF strip to each side of the paper-pieced unit. Press the seams toward the inner borders.

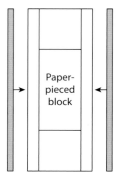

Fabric B 1½″ × WOF strips

2 Trim the excess fabric, as in Construct the Center Unit, Step 3 (at left).

ADD THE OUTER SECTIONS

1 With right sides together, pin the 30½″ edge of the Fabric C 10″ × 30½″ rectangle to the left edge of the paper-pieced unit. Sew in place. Press the seam toward the inner border.

2 Repeat Step 1, sewing the Fabric C 24″ × 30½″ rectangle to the right edge.

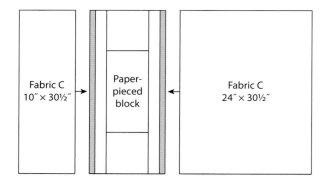

QUILTING

1 Layer the backing (right side facing down), batting, and quilt top (right side facing up).

2 Pin together all 3 layers and quilt as desired.

BINDING

Follow the instructions in Lap Quilt, Binding (page 23), using the Fabric C binding strips.

FINISHING

Hand sew any desired buttons on through all thicknesses.

Backpack

FINISHED BACKPACK: 16″ wide × 17″ high × 3″ deep

Materials

Refer to your chosen block's materials list for additional paper-piecing and embellishment requirements. All block background fabric amounts are included in this materials list.

Fabric A: ⅝ yard for main fabric (using a rectangular 8″ × 15½″ block) *or* ¾ yard (using an optional 8″ block)

Fabric B: ¾ yard for lining

Fabric C: ¼ yard for background (using a rectangular 8″ × 15½″ block) *or* 1 fat eighth 9″ × 21″ (using an optional 8″ block)

Fabric D: ⅝ yard (Muslin is recommended.)

Fusible fleece: ⅝ yard

Fusible interfacing: ½ yard (Pellon 809 Décor-Bond is recommended.)

Grommets (10): 12 mm

Grosgrain ribbon: 1″ wide, 2½ yards

Chalk pencil

Cutting

WOF = width of fabric. Fold fabric selvage to selvage.

Fabric A

- Cut 1 strip 17½″ × WOF. Subcut into:

  1 rectangle 15½″ × 17½″ for back

  2 strips 3¾″ × 17½″ for top bands

  2 rectangles 5½″ × 15½″ for front side panels

Fabric B

- Cut 1 strip 16½″ × WOF. Subcut into 2 rectangles 17½″ × 16½″ for lining.

- Cut 1 strip 9″ × WOF. Subcut into 2 squares 9″ × 9″ for inside pocket.

Fabric D

- Cut 1 square 18″ × 18″.

Fusible fleece

- Cut 1 square 18″ × 18″.

Fusible interfacing

- Cut 2 strips 3½″ × 17½″.

- Cut 1 square 9″ × 9″.

Sewing

Use ¼" seams throughout, unless otherwise directed.

PAPER-PIECED BLOCK

Refer to Paper-Piecing Basics (page 7) as needed. Refer to Block Patterns (page 44) to choose a block.

1 Paper piece 1 selected rectangular block using Fabric C for the background fabric. If you prefer using a square paper-pieced block, sew an 8″ × 8″ square of Fabric A to the bottom of the finished square block. (You will need ¾ yard of Fabric A.)

2 Add any necessary embroidery. Do not add any buttons at this time, but mark their placement.

ASSEMBLE AND QUILT THE FRONT UNIT

1 Sew a Fabric A 5½″ × 15½″ rectangle to each side of the paper-pieced block. Press the seam allowance toward Fabric A. Remove the paper from the back of the paper-pieced block.

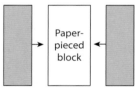

Sew rectangles to both sides of paper-pieced block.

2 Steam press the fusible fleece to the back of the front unit. Be cautious with the ironing, as the fusible fleece is larger than the front unit and will be trimmed later.

3 Pin the Fabric D 18″ square to the back of the fusible fleece.

4 Quilt as desired. *Note:* Quilting is always recommended over any paper-pieced image so none of the pieces will distort when laundering.

5 Trim the front unit to 17½″ × 15½″.

6 Add any necessary buttons.

ADD THE TOP BANDS

1 On the wrong side of each Fabric A 3¾″ × 17½″ strip, steam press the fusible interfacing strip, aligning it to a long edge.

2 Press the non-interfaced edge under ¼″ on both bands.

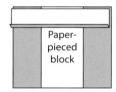

Top band with fusible interfacing pressed in place

3 With right sides together, sew the interfaced edge of the top band to the top of the backpack front and back. The 17½″ edge is the top. Press the seam allowance toward the bands.

Sew a band to the top of both the front and back.

ASSEMBLE THE OUTSIDE OF THE BACKPACK

1 With right sides together, pin the front to the back, matching the seamlines under the bands, opening the ¼″ pressed edge.

2 Sew around the sides and bottom of the backpack. Trim the bottom corners. Turn the backpack right side out.

3 Turn the ¼″ pressed edge of the top band back under, and re-press.

4 Fold the band in half so the pressed edge reaches the stitching. Press, but do not pin.

PREPARE THE INSIDE POCKET

1 Steam press the fusible interfacing to the wrong side of 1 Fabric B 9″ × 9″ square.

2 Pin the 2 squares right sides together. Sew all the way around, leaving a 5″ turning hole.

5″ turning hole

3 Turn pocket right side out. Poke the corners square. Press flat.

SEW THE INSIDE POCKET TO THE LINING

1 With the turning hole at the bottom, pin the pocket to the right side of a Fabric B 16½″ × 17½″ rectangle. The 17½″ edges should be at the top and bottom. Make sure the pocket will open to the top. Place the pocket 4″ from the top and 4½″ from each side.

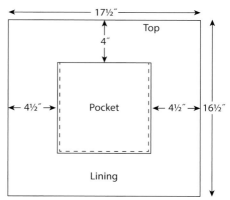

Pocket placement on lining

2 Stitch around 3 sides of the pocket ⅛″ from the edges, leaving the top of the pocket open. Backtack at the top corners.

ADD THE LINING TO THE BACKPACK

1 With right sides together, pin together the 2 Fabric B lining pieces, leaving the top open. Stitch. *Do not turn right side out.*

2 Slide the lining inside the main body, matching the side seams. Fold the pressed edge of the top band over the raw edges of the lining. Pin in place. Stitch the lining in place, stitching close to the folded edge. It is easier to stitch from the inside of the backpack.

Stitch top band in place over lining.

ADD THE GROMMETS

1 Place a pin in the center front of the top band. Use a chalk pencil to mark the placement of the first 2 grommets, 2¼″ on each side of the center front. Continue to mark the placement of 6 more grommets, each spaced approximately 4¼″ apart around the top band.

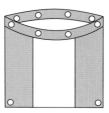

2 Follow the manufacturer's instructions to attach each grommet. There should be 8 total grommets along the top band.

3 Mark the placement of 1 grommet in each of the 2 bottom corners of the backpack, about 1″ from the edges through all thicknesses. Insert the grommets.

ADD THE GROSGRAIN RIBBON

Tie an end of the 2½ yards of grosgrain ribbon into the bottom corner grommet. Thread the ribbon through the 8 grommets in the top band, following the arrows as shown. Adjust the length of the ribbon as needed for the backpack's wearer. Tie the end of the ribbon into the remaining bottom corner.

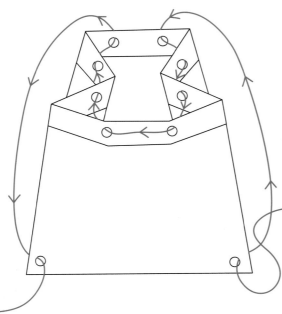

Thread ribbon through 10 grommets in this direction, starting and ending in bottom corners.

Wallhanging

FINISHED WALLHANGING: 16″ × 23½″

Materials

Refer to your chosen block's materials list for additional paper-piecing and embellishment requirements.

Fabric A: ⅓ yard for inner and outer borders

Fabric B: ¼ yard for middle border

Fabric C: ¼ yard for binding

Fabric D: ⅞ yard for backing and hanger

Batting: 20″ × 28″

Cutting

WOF = width of fabric. Fold fabric selvage to selvage, unless otherwise directed.

Fabric A

• Cut 4 strips 1½″ × WOF.

  From 2 strips, subcut into 2 strips 1½″ × 15½″ and 2 strips 1½″ × 10″.

  From *each of* 2 strips, subcut into 1 strip 1½″ × 21½″ and 1 strip 1½″ × 16″.

• Cut 1 strip 2½″ × WOF. Subcut into 4 corner squares 2½″ × 2½″.

Fabric B

• Cut 2 strips 2½″ × WOF. Subcut into 2 strips 2½″ × 17¼″ and 2 strips 2½″ × 10″.

Fabric C

• Cut 2 strips 2½″ × WOF.

Fabric D

Open fabric flat.

• Cut 1 strip 28″ × WOF. Subcut into:

  1 rectangle 20″ × 28″ for backing

  1 rectangle 8½″ × 21″ for horizontal hanger *or* 1 rectangle 8½″ × 15″ for vertical hanger

Sewing

Use ¼″ seams throughout, unless otherwise directed.

PAPER-PIECED BLOCKS

Refer to Paper-Piecing Basics (page 7) as needed. Refer to Block Patterns (page 44) to choose a block.

1 Paper piece 1 selected rectangular block.

2 Add any necessary embroidery. Do not add any buttons at this time, but mark their placement.

ADD THE INNER BORDER

1 Sew the Fabric A 1½″ × 15½″ strips to the side edges of the paper-pieced block. Press the seams toward the border.

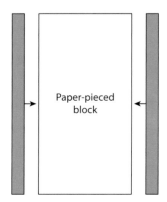

Paper-pieced block

2 Sew a Fabric A 1½″ × 10″ strip to the remaining 2 sides of the paper-pieced block. Press the seams toward the border.

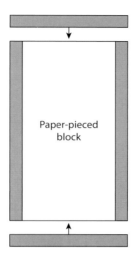

ADD THE MIDDLE BORDER

1 Sew the Fabric B 2½″ × 17½″ strips to the side edges of the unit. Press the seams toward the middle borders.

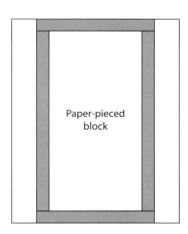

2 Sew a Fabric A 2½″ × 2½″ corner square to each end of a Fabric B 2½″ × 10″ strip. Press the seams toward the middle borders. Make 2 middle borders with corner squares.

3 Pin a prepared middle border to a short end of the quilt, matching the seams. Sew in place. Press the seam toward the middle border. Repeat with the second middle border with corner squares.

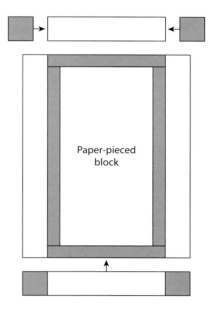

ADD THE OUTER BORDER

1 Sew the Fabric A 1½″ × 21½″ strips to the side edges of the unit. Press the seams toward the outer border.

2 Sew the Fabric A 1½″ × 16″ strips to the remaining ends of the unit. Press the seams toward the outer border.

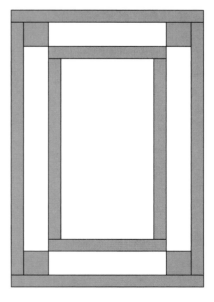

QUILTING

1 Remove the paper from the back of the paper-pieced block.

2 Layer the Fabric D backing (right side facing down), batting, and wallhanging (right side facing up).

3 Pin together all 3 layers, and quilt as desired.

BINDING

Follow the instructions in Lap Quilt, Binding (page 23), using the 2 Fabric C 2½" × WOF strips.

FINISHING

Hand sew any desired buttons on through all thicknesses.

Hanger Option 1: Vertical Wallhanging

1 Press under ¼" on each 8½" edge of the Fabric C 8½" × 15" rectangle. Press under another ½". Sew these hems in place close to the pressed edges.

2 With right sides together, sew together the long edges of Fabric C to form a tube. Turn the tube right side out and press it flat, centering the seam down the center back of the hanger.

3 On the back of the wallhanging, pin the tube to the top of the wallhanging directly beneath the binding. Hand stitch the hanger in place all the way around, leaving the short ends of the tube open.

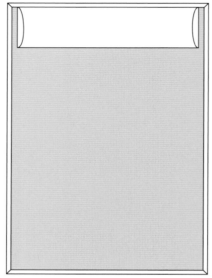

Vertical wallhanging with hanger on back

Hanger Option 2: Horizontal Wallhanging

Follow Hanger Option 1: Vertical Wallhanging, Steps 1–3 (at left), but in this case, use the Fabric C 8½" × 21" rectangle. Hem the same 8½" edges.

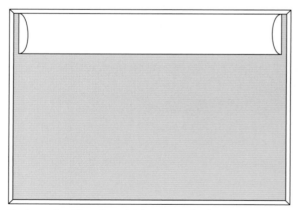

Horizontal wallhanging with hanger on back

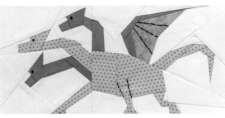

Block Patterns

Block sizes   All the blocks are two-part rectangular blocks except for Unicorn 1 (next page, which is a one-part square block) and Castle (pages 74–78, which can be made as a one-part square block, a two-part rectangular block, or a four-part large square block).

Materials needed   All the materials needed for a complete block are listed under Part 1. If you choose to make only one part of a completed block, check the block photos for the actual fabrics needed.

More detailed instructions   Refer to Paper-Piecing Basics (page 7) as needed for detailed instructions when making the blocks.

Foundation papers and buttons   Refer to the specific project instructions about when to remove foundation papers and attach buttons. Any hand sewing included in the following block instructions is meant to be done with foundation papers attached.

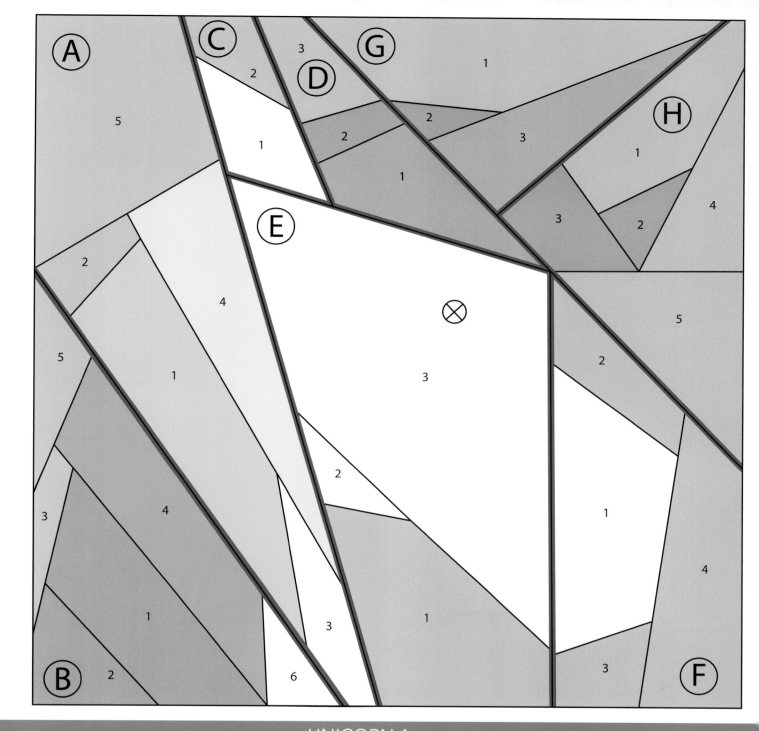

UNICORN 1

Materials

- Large scrap of dark blue, at least 9″ × 11″
- Scraps of white, orange, pink, yellow, green, blue, purple, and stripe
- 1 black ¼″ button for eye

Directions

1. Make 3 copies of the pattern (A/D/F, B/G/E, C/H).

2. Cut around each segment, adding ¼″ seam allowances.

3. Paper piece each segment.

4. Connect the segments: A to B; C to D to E to F; G to H; A/B to C/D/E/F to G/H.

5. Trim the block to 8″ × 8″.

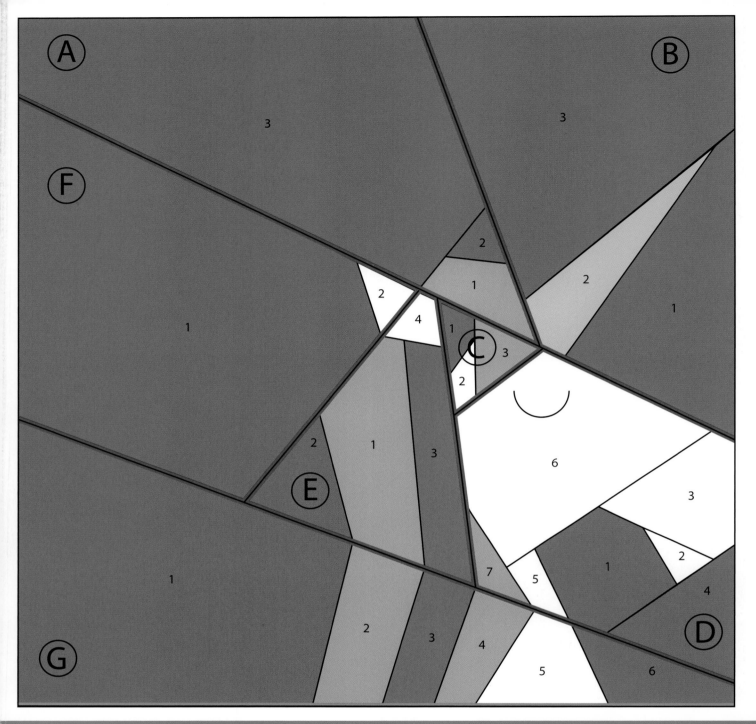

UNICORN 2, PART 1

Materials

- 1 fat eighth 9″ × 21″ of black
- Scraps of white, pink, purple, and gold
- Black embroidery floss

Directions

1. Make 4 copies of the pattern (A/G, B/E, C, D/F).

2. Cut around each segment, adding ¼″ seam allowances.

3. Paper piece each segment.

4. Connect the segments: A to B; C to D to E to F; A/B to C/D/E/F to G.

5. Trim ¼″ from the blue line.

6. Embroider the eye.

7. Continue to Unicorn 2, Part 2 (next page).

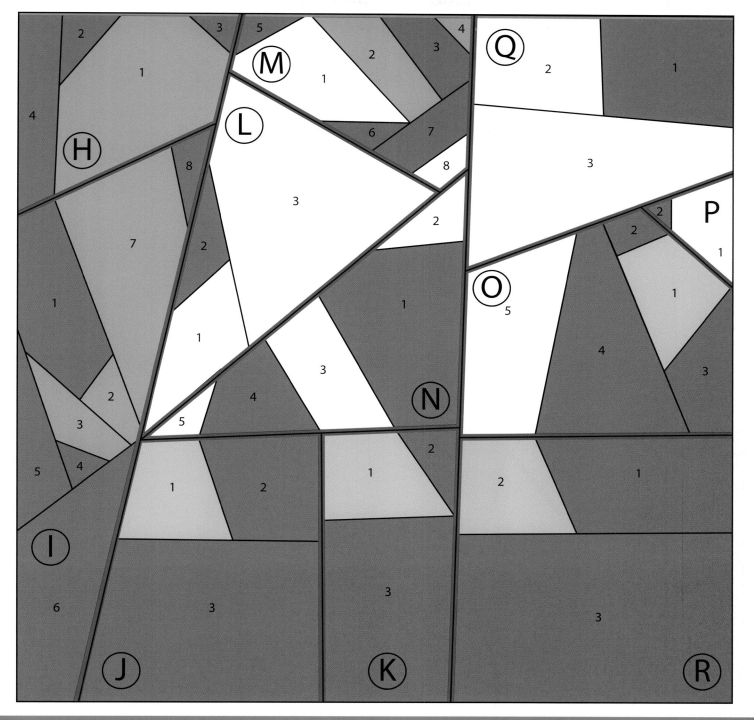

UNICORN 2, PART 2

Directions

1. Make 5 copies of the pattern (M/J, H/N/P, L/Q/R, I/O, K).

2. Cut around each segment, adding ¼" seam allowances.

3. Paper piece each segment.

4. Connect the segments: H to I; J to K; L to M to N; J/K to L/M/N; O to P to Q to R; H/I to J/K/L/M/N to O/P/Q/R.

5. Trim ¼" from the blue line. Match and sew Part 1 to Part 2 on the blue lines.

6. Trim the block to 8" × 15½".

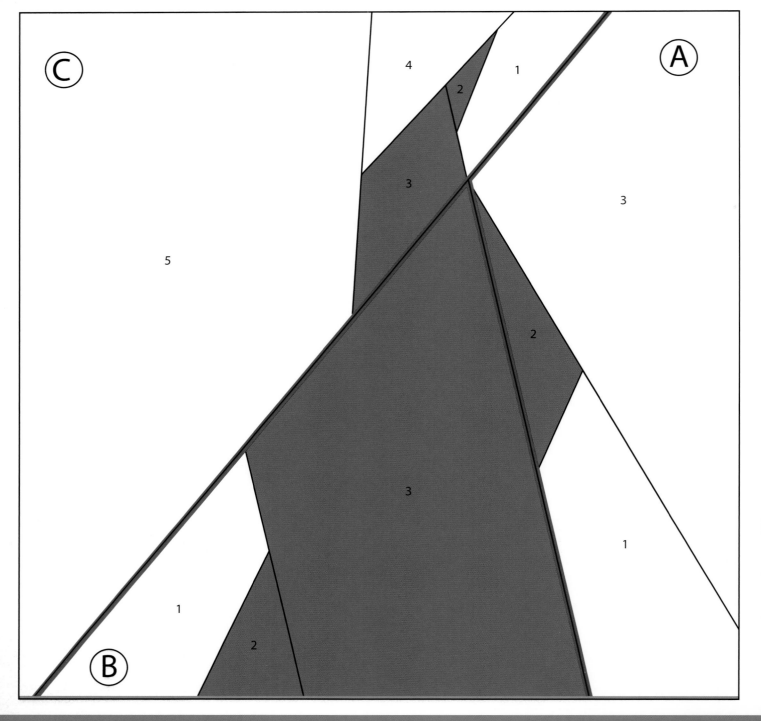

GNOME, PART 1

Materials

- 1 fat eighth 9″ × 21″ of gray
- Scraps of brown, dark brown, white, blue, and peach
- Small bit of stuffing

Directions

1. Make 3 copies of the pattern (A, B, C).

2. Cut around each segment, adding ¼″ seam allowances.

3. Paper piece each segment.

4. Connect the segments: A to B; A/B to C.

5. Trim ¼″ from the blue line.

6. Continue to Gnome, Part 2 (next page).

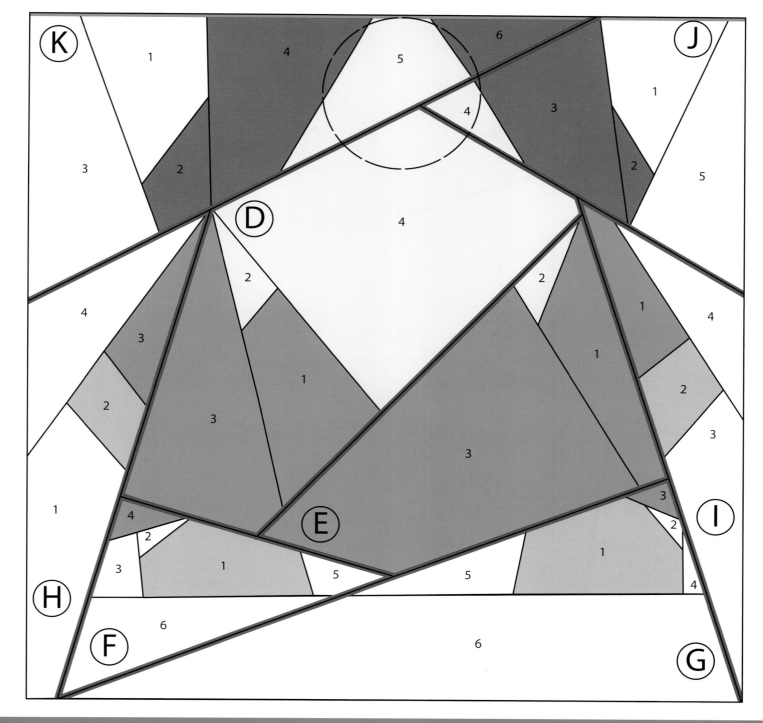

GNOME, PART 2

Directions

1. Make 4 copies of the pattern (K/E, J/H, D/G, F/I).

2. Cut around each segment, adding ¼″ seam allowances.

3. Paper piece each segment.

4. Connect the segments: D to E to F to G to H to I to J to K.

5. Trim ¼″ from the blue line. Match and sew
Part 1 to Part 2 on the blue lines.

6. Trim the block to 8″ × 15½″.

7. To complete the Gnome block, see Gnome Block Finishing (page 78).

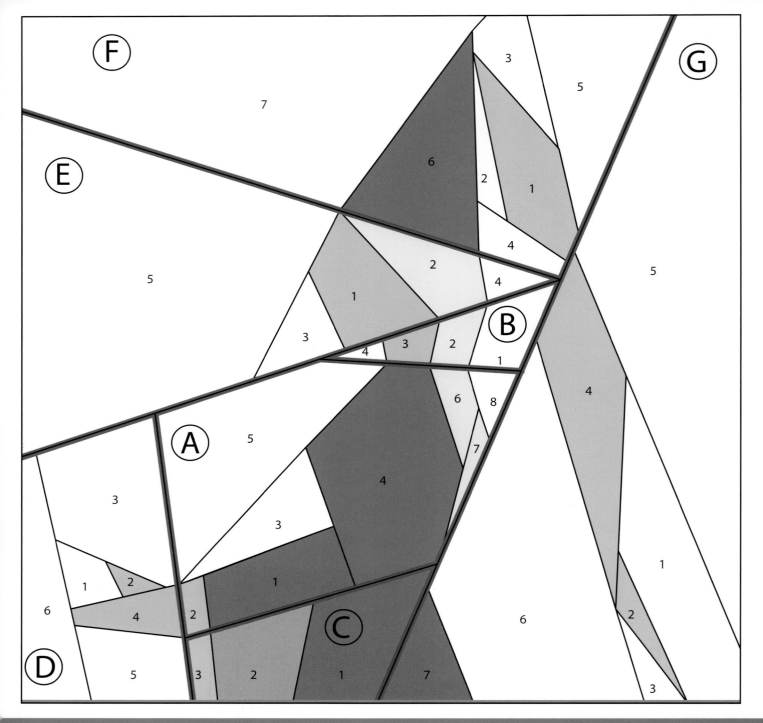

Materials

- 1 fat eighth 9″ × 21″ of white
- Scraps of gold, yellow, peach, light purple, and dark purple

Directions

1. Make 4 copies of the pattern (A/F, B/C, D/G, E).

2. Cut around each segment, adding ¼″ seam allowances.

3. Paper piece each segment.

4. Connect the segments: A to B to C to D to E to F to G.

5. Trim ¼″ from the blue line.

6. Continue to Princess, Part 2 (next page).

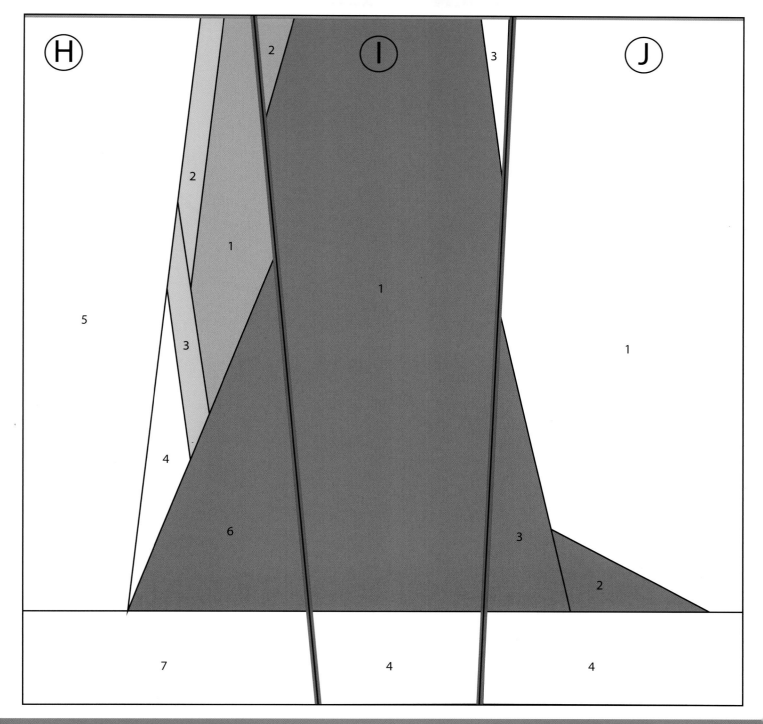

PRINCESS, PART 2

Directions

1. Make 2 copies of the pattern (H/J, I).

2. Cut around each segment, adding ¼" seam allowances.

3. Paper piece each segment.

4. Connect the segments: H to I to J.

5. Trim ¼" from the blue line. Match and sew Part 1 to Part 2 on the blue lines.

6. Trim the block to 8" × 15½".

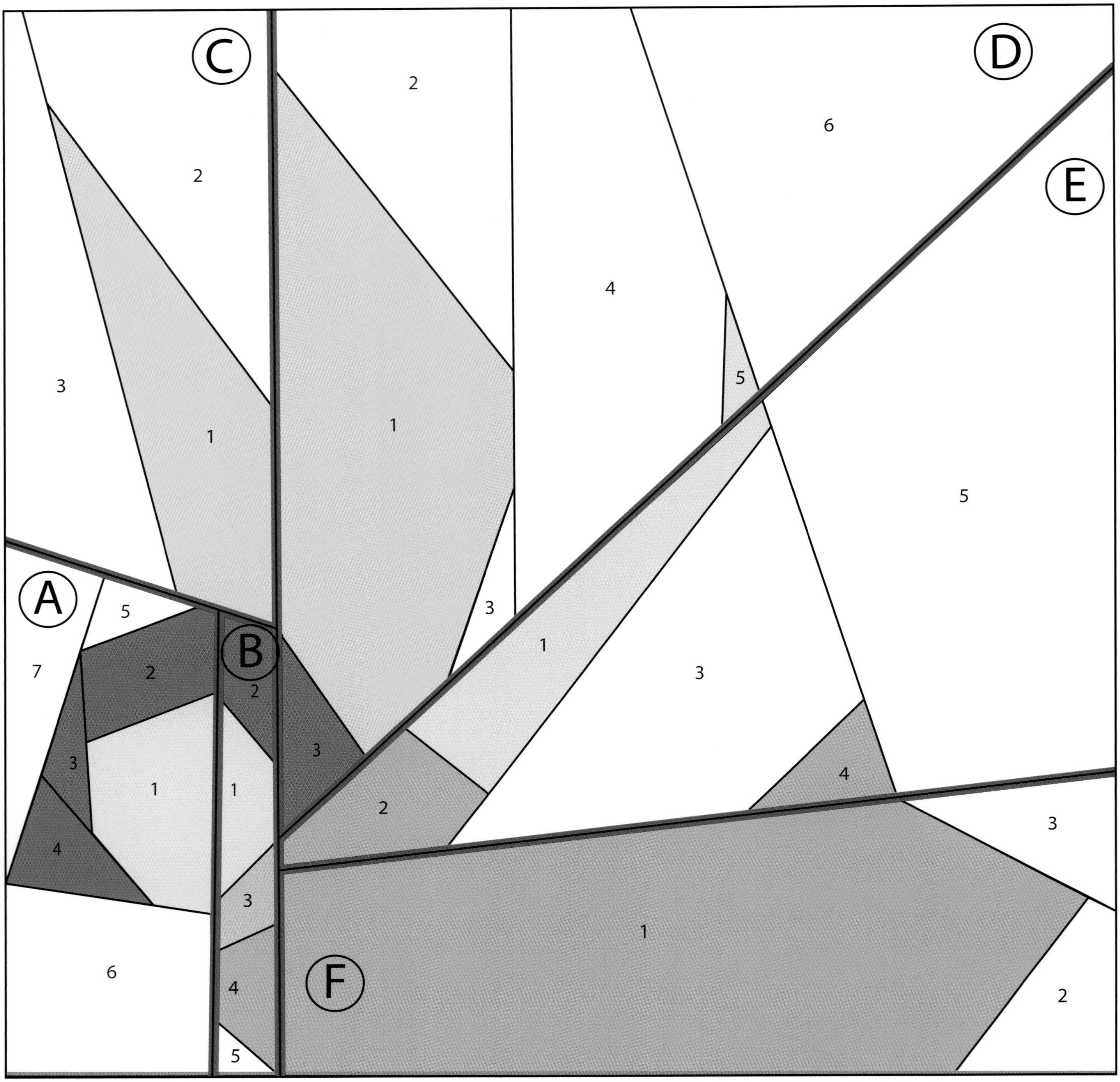

FAIRY, PART 1

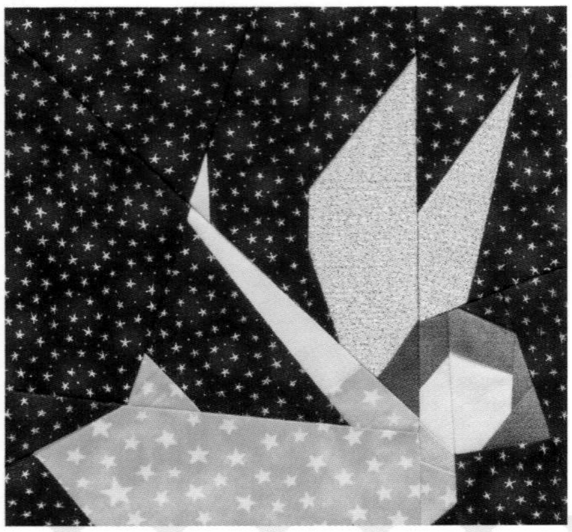

Materials

- 1 fat eighth 9″ × 21″ of purple
- Scraps of gold, light peach, dark peach, green, and brown
- Gold metallic embroidery floss/thread
- Silver sequin

Directions

1. Make 3 copies of the pattern (A/D/F, C/E, B).
2. Cut around each segment, adding ¼″ seam allowances.
3. Paper piece each segment.
4. Connect the segments: A to B to C; D to E to F; A/B/C to D/E/F.
5. Trim ¼″ from the blue line.
6. Continue to Fairy, Part 2 (next page).

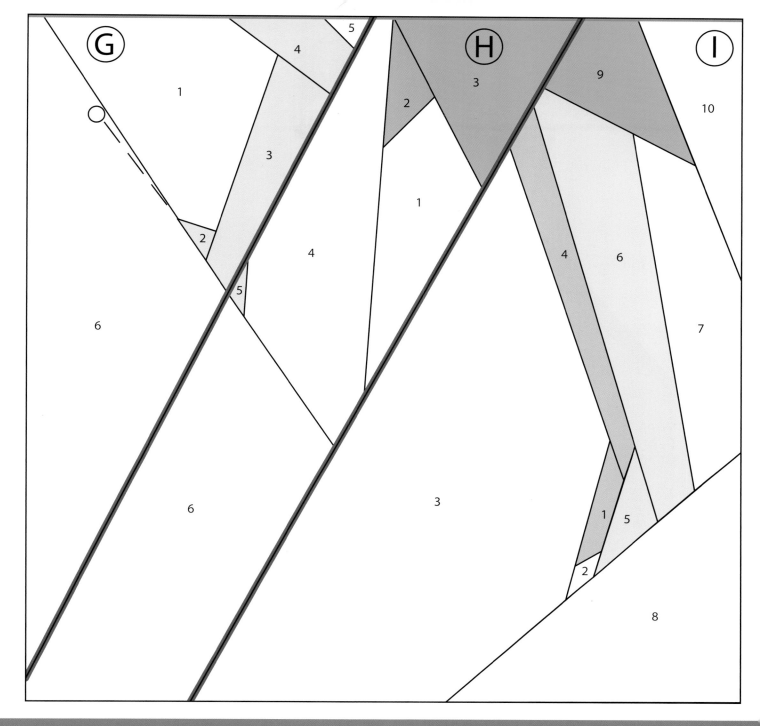

Directions

1. Make 2 copies of the pattern (G/I, H).

2. Cut around each segment, adding ¼″ seam allowances.

3. Paper piece each segment.

4. Connect the segments: G to H to I.

5. Trim ¼″ from the blue line. Match and sew Part 1 to Part 2 on the blue lines.

6. Trim the block to 8″ × 15½″.

7. Embroider the wand. Hand sew a ¼″ sequin to the end of the wand.

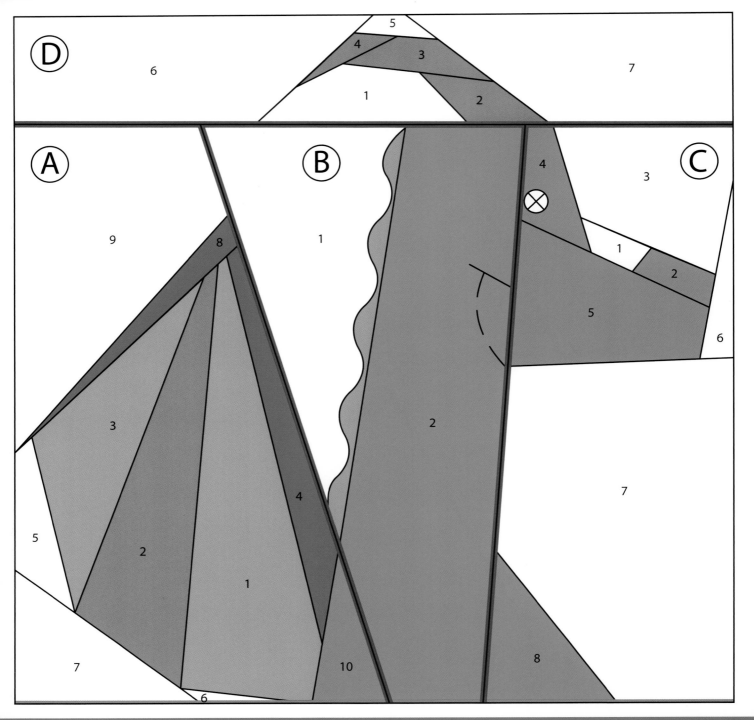

DRAGON 1, PART 1

Materials

- 1 fat eighth 9″ × 21″ of white
- Scraps of green, dark green, light orange, and dark orange
- 2 pieces of 5″ orange rickrack
- 1 black ¼″ button for eye
- Black embroidery floss

Directions

1. Make 3 copies of the pattern (A/C, B, D).

2. Cut around each segment, adding ¼″ seam allowances.

3. Paper piece each segment. The orange rickrack is set into the paper-pieced seam of Segment B as indicated on the pattern.

4. Connect the segments: A to B to C; A/B/C to D.

5. Trim ¼″ from the blue line.

6. Embroider the mouth.

7. Continue to Dragon 1, Part 2 (next page).

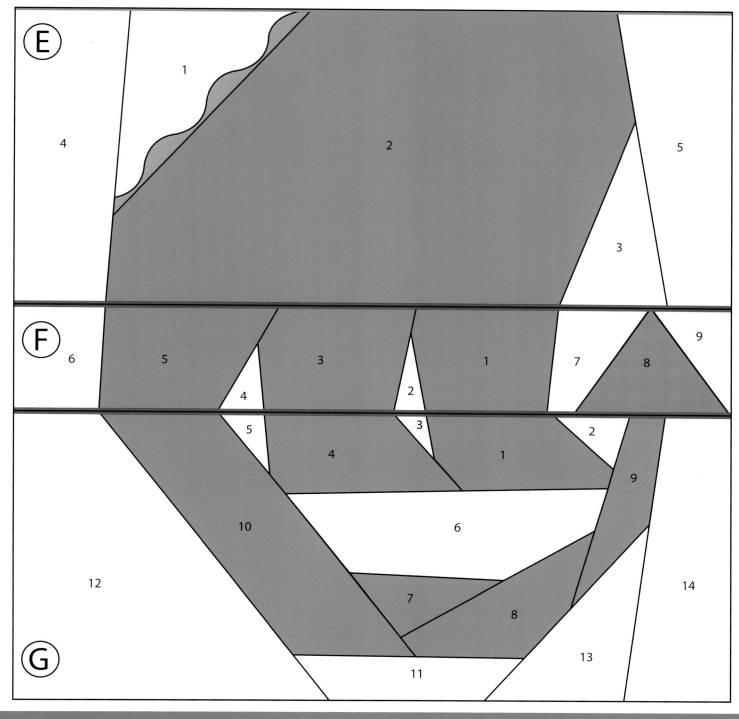

DRAGON 1, PART 2

Directions

1. Make 2 copies of the pattern (E/G, F).

2. Cut around each segment, adding ¼" seam allowances.

3. Paper piece each segment. The orange rickrack is set into the paper-pieced seam of Segment E as indicated on the pattern.

4. Connect the segments: E to F to G.

5. Trim ¼" from the blue line. Match and sew Part 1 to Part 2 on the blue lines.

6. Trim the block to 8" × 15½".

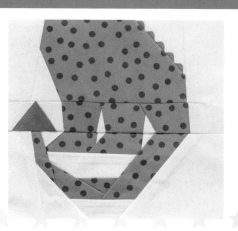

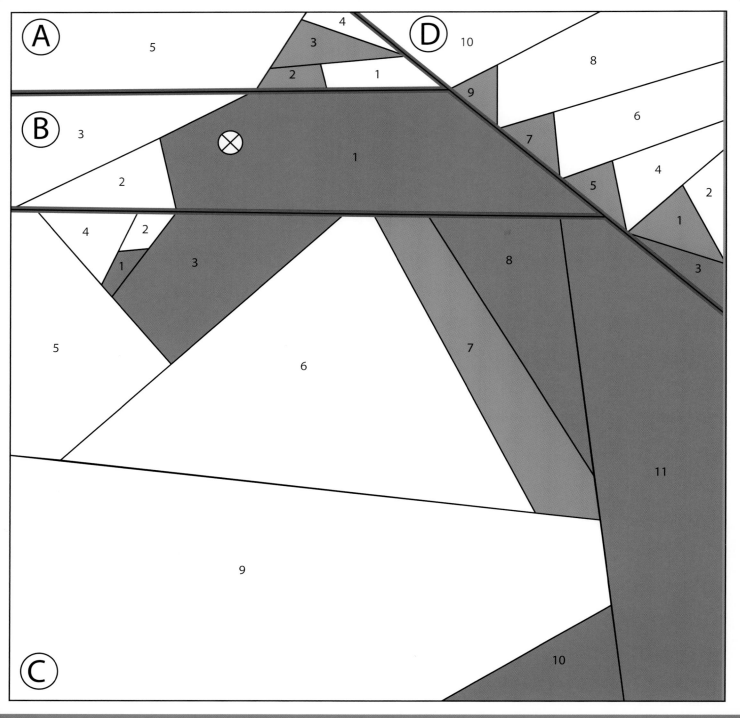

DRAGON 2, PART 1

Materials

- 1 fat eighth 9″ × 21″ of white
- Scraps of purple, light orange, dark orange, and orange stripe
- 1 white ⅛″ button for eye

Directions

1. Make 3 copies of the pattern (A/C, B, D).

2. Cut around each segment, adding ¼″ seam allowances.

3. Paper piece each segment.

4. Connect the segments: A to B to C; A/B/C to D.

5. Trim ¼″ from the blue line.

6. Continue to Dragon 2, Part 2 (next page).

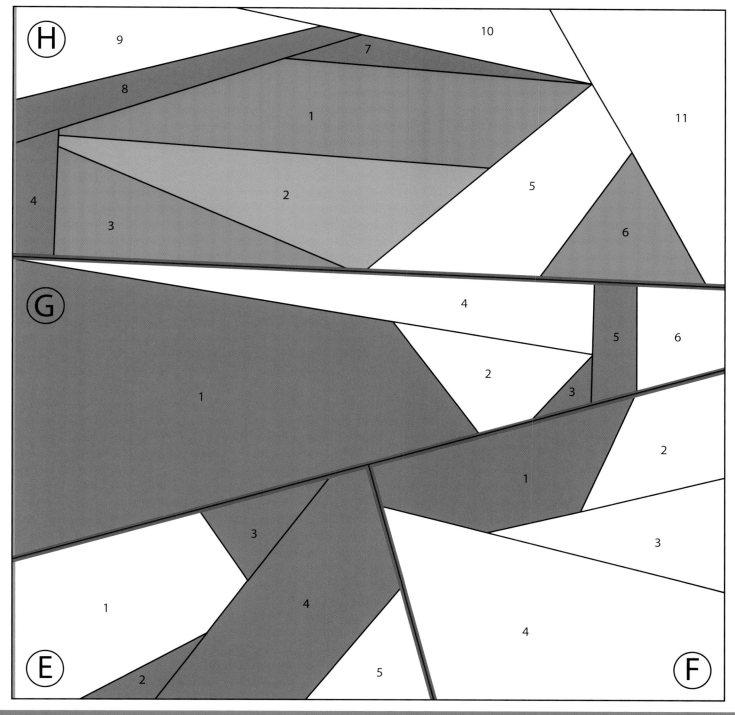

DRAGON 2, PART 2

Directions

1. Make 3 copies of the pattern (E/H, F, G).

2. Cut around each segment, adding ¼″ seam allowances.

3. Paper piece each segment.

4. Connect the segments: E to F to G to H.

5. Trim ¼″ from the blue line. Match and sew Part 1 to Part 2 on the blue lines.

6. Trim the block to 8″ × 15½″.

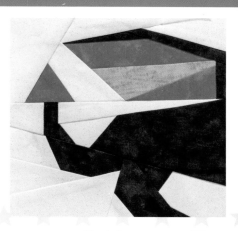

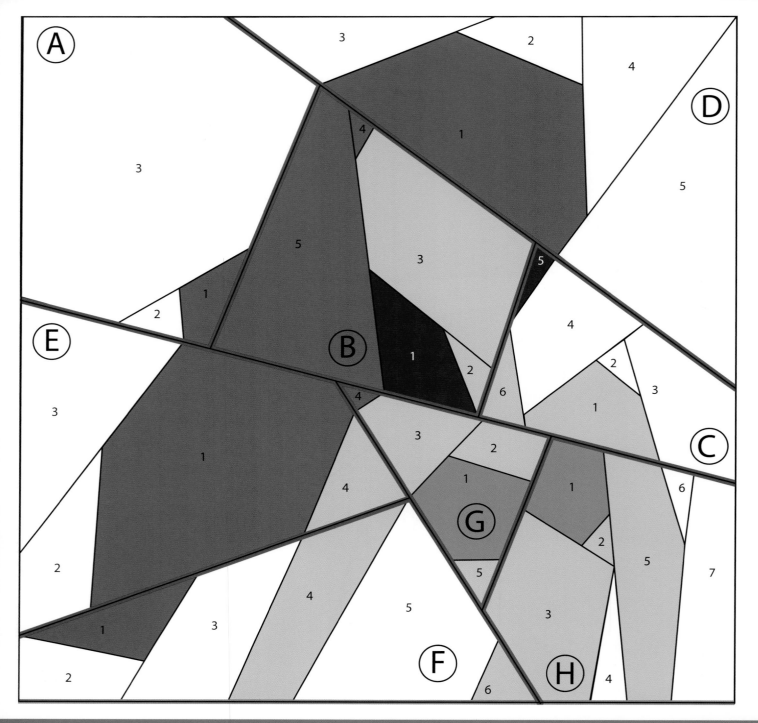

MERMAID, PART 1

Materials

- 1 fat eighth 9″ × 21″ of white
- Scraps of peach, light blue, medium blue, blue stripe, light brown, and dark brown

Directions

1. Make 4 copies of the pattern (A/C/F, B/H, D/E, G).

2. Cut around each segment, adding ¼″ seam allowances.

3. Paper piece each segment.

4. Connect the segments: A to B to C to D; E to F; G to H; E/F to G/H; A/B/C/D to E/F/G/H.

5. Trim ¼″ from the blue line.

6. Continue to Mermaid, Part 2 (next page).

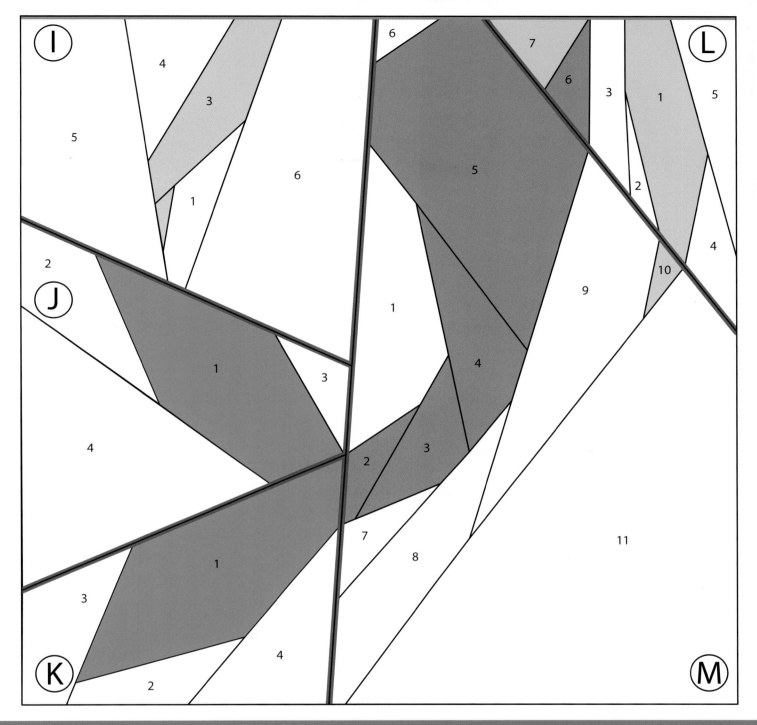

MERMAID, PART 2

Directions

1. Make 3 copies of the pattern (I/K/L, J, M).

2. Cut around each segment, adding ¼" seam allowances.

3. Paper piece each segment.

4. Connect the segments: I to J to K; L to M; I/J/K to L/M.

5. Trim ¼" from the blue line. Match and sew Part 1 to Part 2 on the blue lines.

6. Trim the block to 8" × 15½"

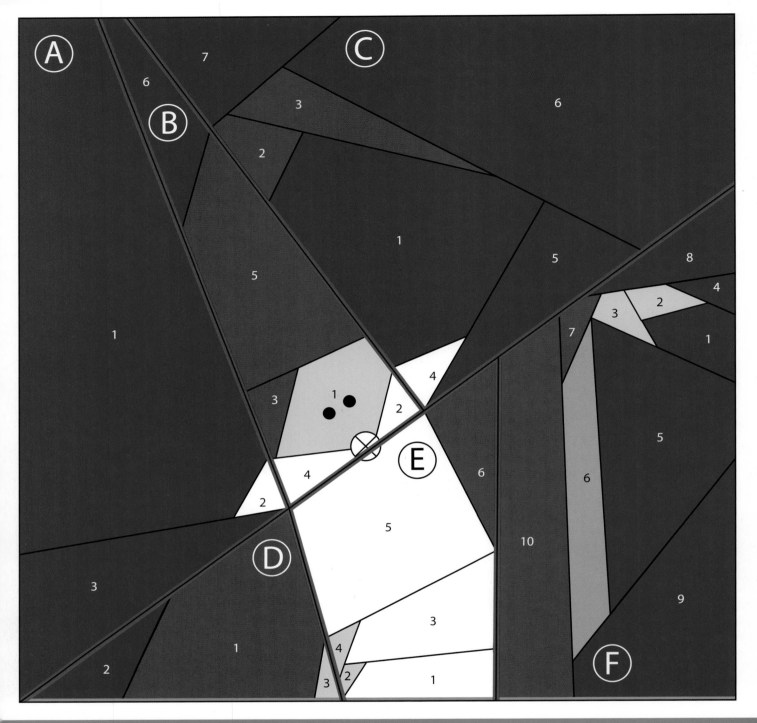

A ⑦ ⑥ B ⑦ C ③ ② ⑥ ① ⑤ ⑤ ⑧ ④ ① ③ ② ④ ③ ① ④ ② ⑤ ④ E ⑥ ⑦ ③ ② ① ④ ⑤ ⑥ ① ⑤ ② D ⑩ ④ ② ③ ① ⑨ F ③

Materials

- 1 fat eighth 9″ × 21″ of blue
- Scraps of peach, black, white, and dark gray
- 1 peach ¼″ button for nose
- Black embroidery floss

Directions

1. Make 4 copies of the pattern (A/C, D/F, B, E).

2. Cut around each segment, adding ¼″ seam allowances.

3. Paper piece each segment.

4. Connect the segments: A to B to C; D to E to F; A/B/C to D/E/F.

5. Trim ¼″ from the blue line.

6. Embroider French knots for the eyes.

7. Continue to Wizard, Part 2 (next page).

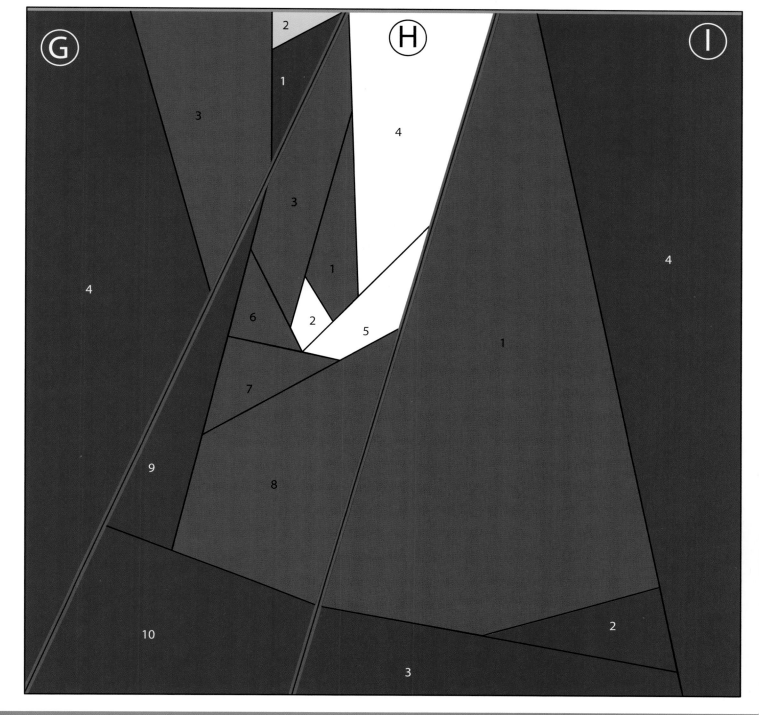

WIZARD, PART 2

Directions

1. Make 2 copies of the pattern (G/I, H).

2. Cut around each segment, adding ¼″ seam allowances.

3. Paper piece each segment.

4. Connect the segments: G to H to I.

5. Trim ¼″ from the blue line. Match and sew Part 1 to Part 2 on the blue lines.

6. Trim the block to 8″ × 15½″.

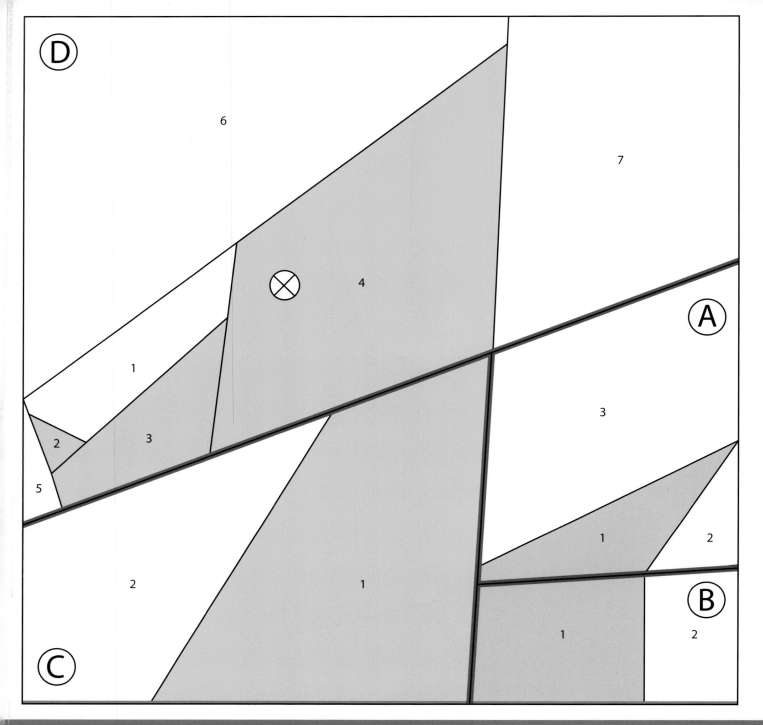

D

6

7

A

1

⊗

4

2

3

3

5

2

1

B

2

2

1

C

1

1

SEAHORSE, PART 1

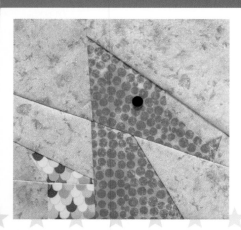

Materials

- 1 fat eighth 9″ × 21″ of light blue
- Scraps of orange and medium blue
- 1 black ¼″ button for eye

Directions

1. Make 3 copies of the pattern (B/D, A, C).

2. Cut around each segment, adding ¼″ seam allowances.

3. Paper piece each segment.

4. Connect the segments: A to B to C; A/B/C to D.

5. Trim ¼″ from the blue line.

6. Continue to Seahorse, Part 2 (next page).

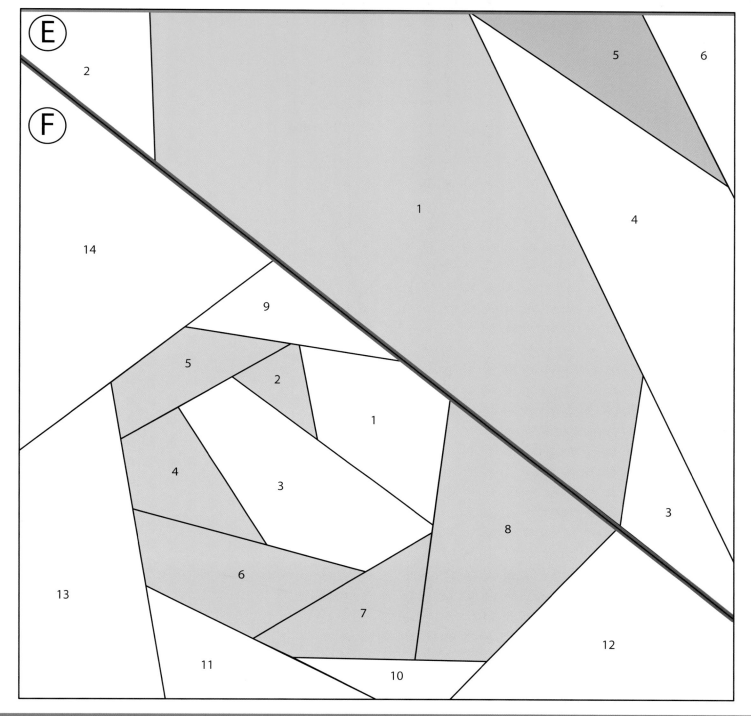

SEAHORSE, PART 2

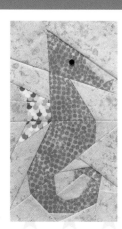

Directions

1. Make 2 copies of the pattern (E, F).

2. Cut around each segment, adding ¼″ seam allowances.

3. Paper piece each segment.

4. Connect the segments: E to F.

5. Trim ¼″ from the blue line. Match and sew Part 1 to Part 2 on the blue lines.

6. Trim the block to 8″ × 15½″.

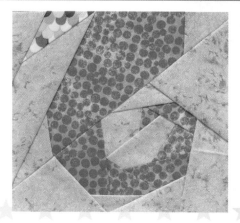

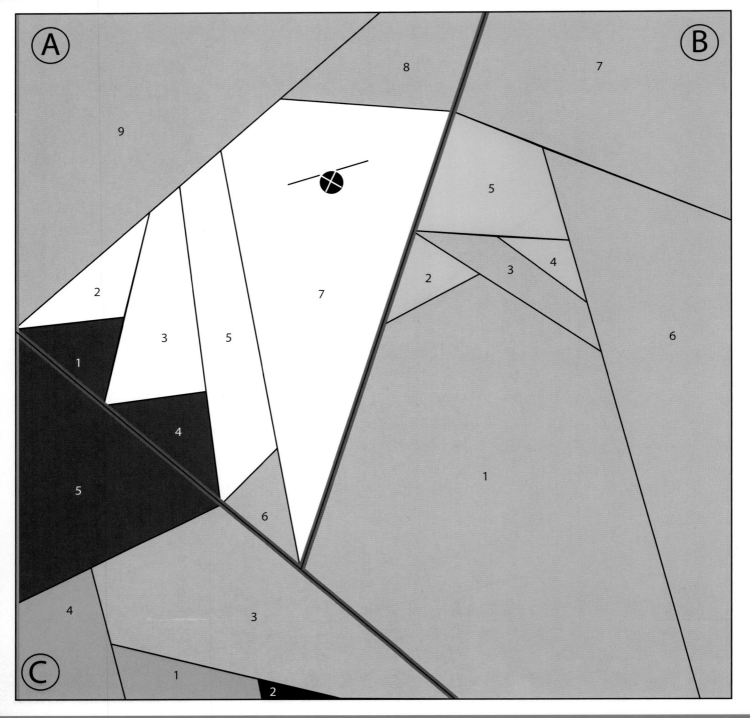

GRYPHON, PART 1

Materials

- 1 fat eighth 9" × 21" of light gray
- Scraps of gold, white, light brown, medium brown, dark brown, and black
- 1 black ¼" button for eye
- Black embroidery floss

Directions

1. Make 3 copies of the pattern (A, B, C).

2. Cut around each segment, adding ¼" seam allowances.

3. Paper piece each segment.

4. Connect the segments: A to B to C.

5. Trim ¼" from the blue line.

6. Embroider the eyebrow.

7. Continue to Gryphon, Part 2 (next page).

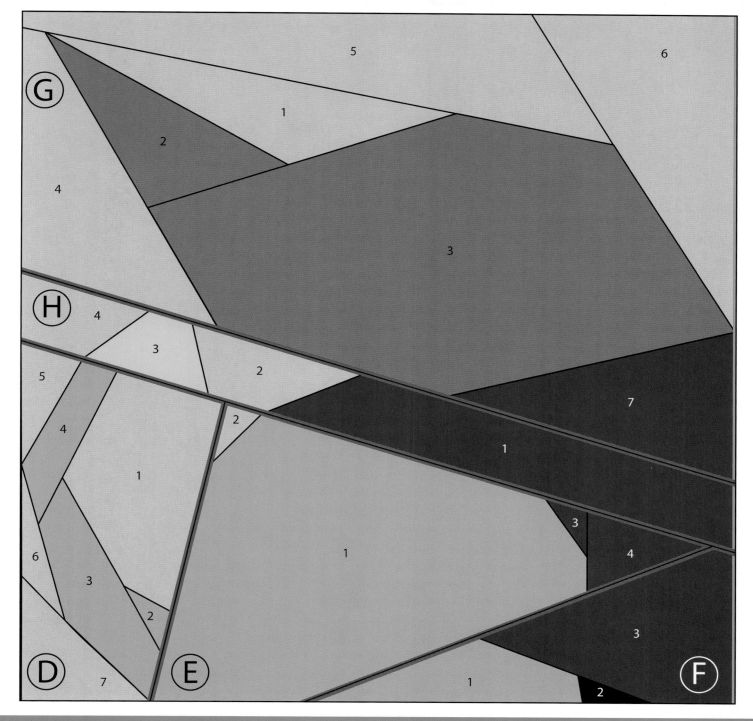

Directions

1. Make 3 copies of the pattern (D/F, E/G, H).

2. Cut around each segment, adding ¼" seam allowances.

3. Paper piece each segment.

4. Connect the segments: D to E to F; G to H; D/E/F to G/H.

5. Trim ¼" from the blue line. Match and sew Part 1 to Part 2 on the blue lines.

6. Trim the block to 8" × 15½".

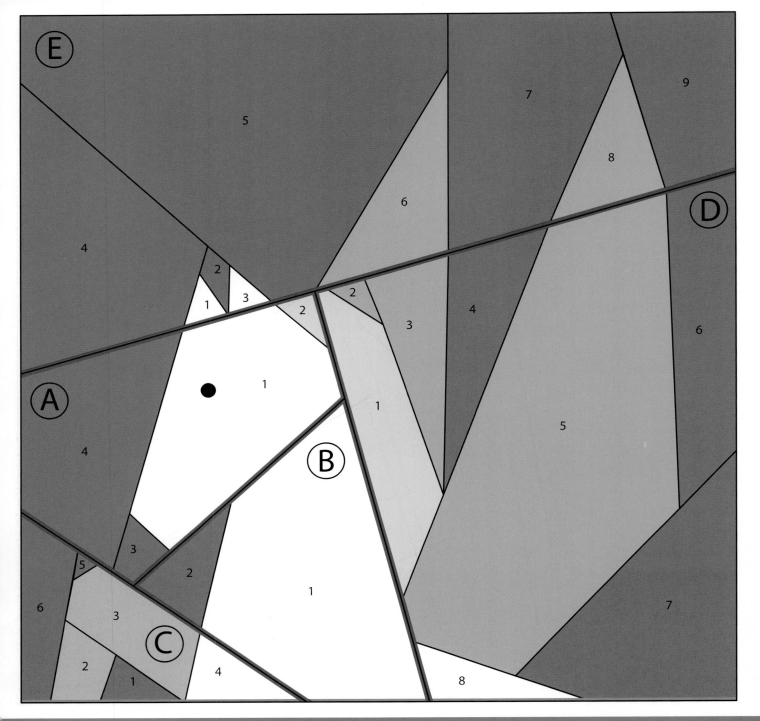

E

5

7

9

4

2

8

D

6

1

3

A

2

2

3

4

1

6

1

4

1

5

B

3

5

2

3

2

6

1

7

C

3

2

4

8

1

PEGASUS, PART 1

Materials

- 1 fat eighth 9″ × 21″ of black
- Scraps of white, pink, light gray, and blue
- Black embroidery floss

Directions

1. Make 3 copies of the pattern (A, B/E, C/D).

2. Cut around each segment, adding ¼″ seam allowances.

3. Paper piece each segment.

4. Connect the segments:
A to B to C to D; A/B/C/D to E.

5. Trim ¼″ from the blue line.

6. Embroider a French knot for the eye.

7. Continue to Pegasus, Part 2 (next page).

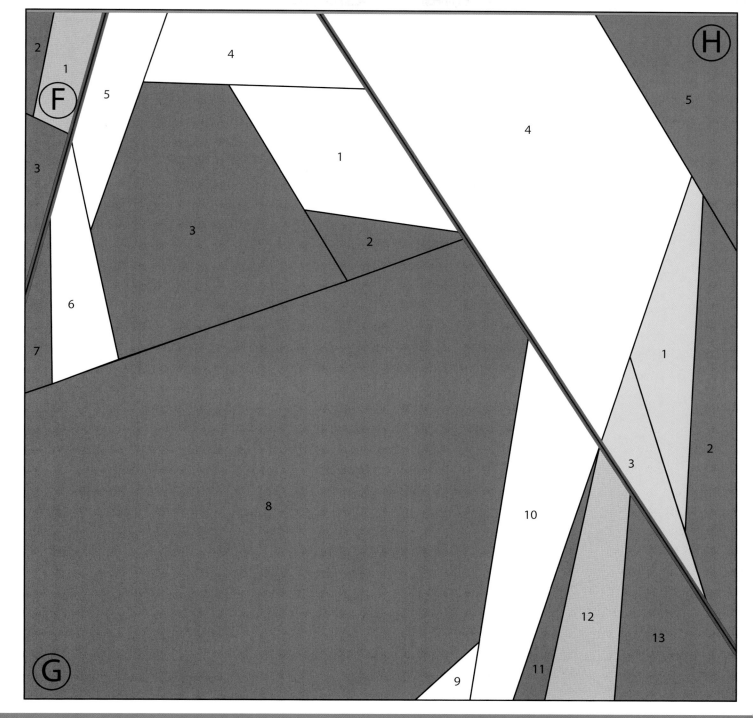

Directions

1. Make 2 copies of the pattern (F/H, G).

2. Cut around each segment, adding ¼" seam allowances.

3. Paper piece each segment.

4. Connect the segments: F to G to H.

5. Trim ¼" from the blue line. Match and sew Part 1 to Part 2 on the blue lines.

6. Trim the block to 8" × 15½".

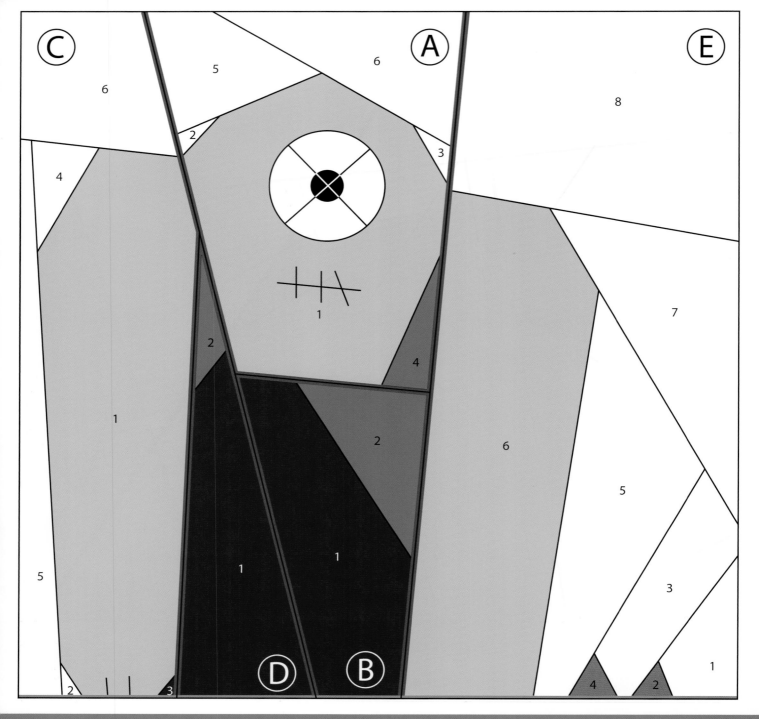

CYCLOPS, PART 1

Materials

- 1 fat eighth 9″ × 21″ of light gray
- Scraps of light green, dark green, light brown, and dark brown
- 1 black ¼″ button and 1 white 1⅛″ button for eye
- Black embroidery floss

Directions

1. Make 3 copies of the pattern (A, C/B, D/E).

2. Cut around each segment, adding ¼″ seam allowances.

3. Paper piece each segment.

4. Connect the segments: A to B; C to D; A/B to C/D to E.

5. Trim ¼″ from the blue line.

6. Embroider the mouth and fingers.

7. Continue to Cyclops, Part 2 (next page).

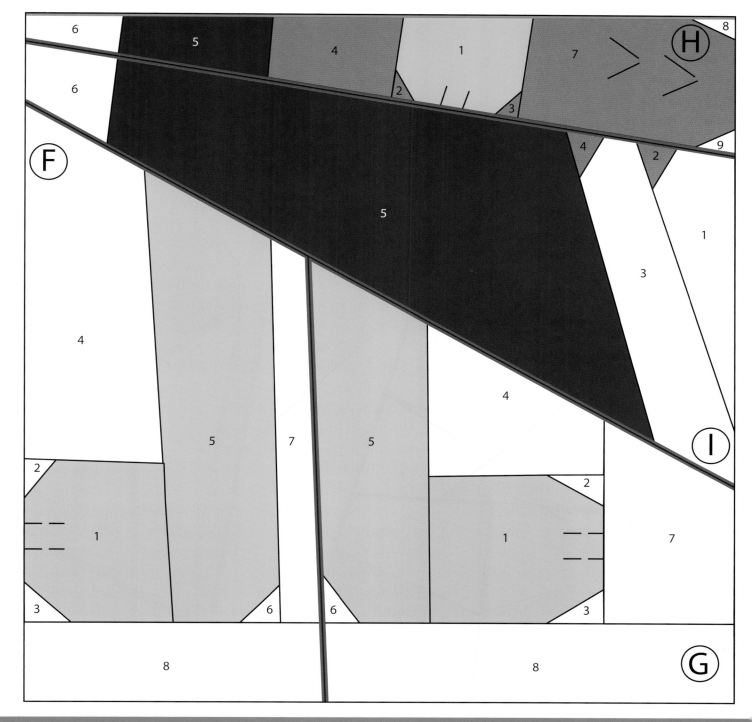

CYCLOPS, PART 2

Directions

1. Make 3 copies of the pattern (F/H, G, I).

2. Cut around each segment, adding ¼″ seam allowances.

3. Paper piece each segment.

4. Connect the segments: F to G; H to I; F/G to H/I.

5. Trim ¼″ from the blue line. Match and sew Part 1 to Part 2 on the blue lines.

6. Trim the block to 8″ × 15½″.

7. Embroider the details on the club, hand, and feet.

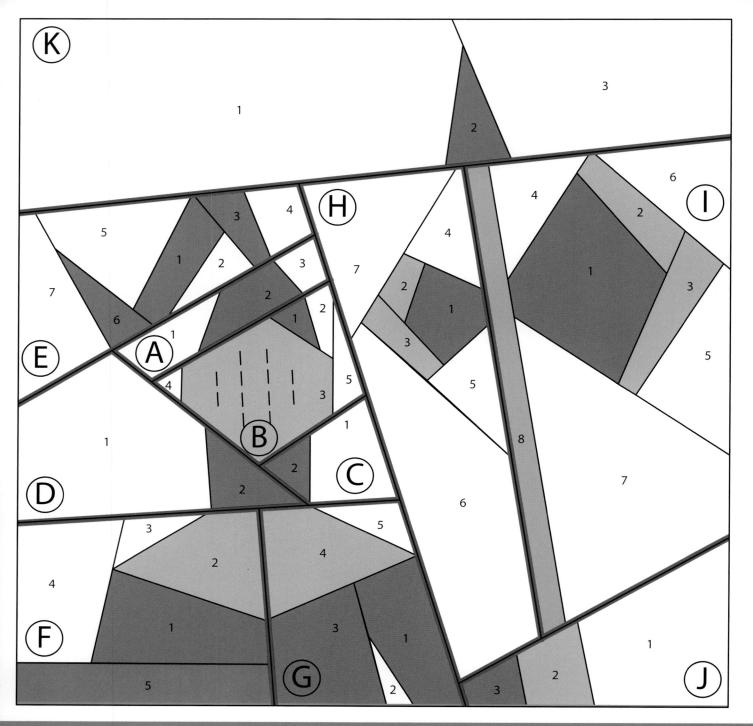

KNIGHT, PART 1

Materials

- 1 fat eighth 9″ × 21″ of light gray
- Scraps of silver, gold, dark gray, red, and brown

Directions

1. Make 4 copies of the pattern (A/F/I, E/C/J, G/B/K, D/H).

2. Cut around each segment, adding ¼″ seam allowances.

3. Paper piece each segment.

4. Connect the segments: A to B to C to D to E; F to G, A/B/C/D/E to F/G; H to I to J; A/B/C/D/E/F/G to H/I/J to K.

5. Trim ¼″ from the blue line.

6. Machine stitch 4 thin rows of black satin stitch on the helmet shield.

7. Continue to Knight, Part 2 (next page).

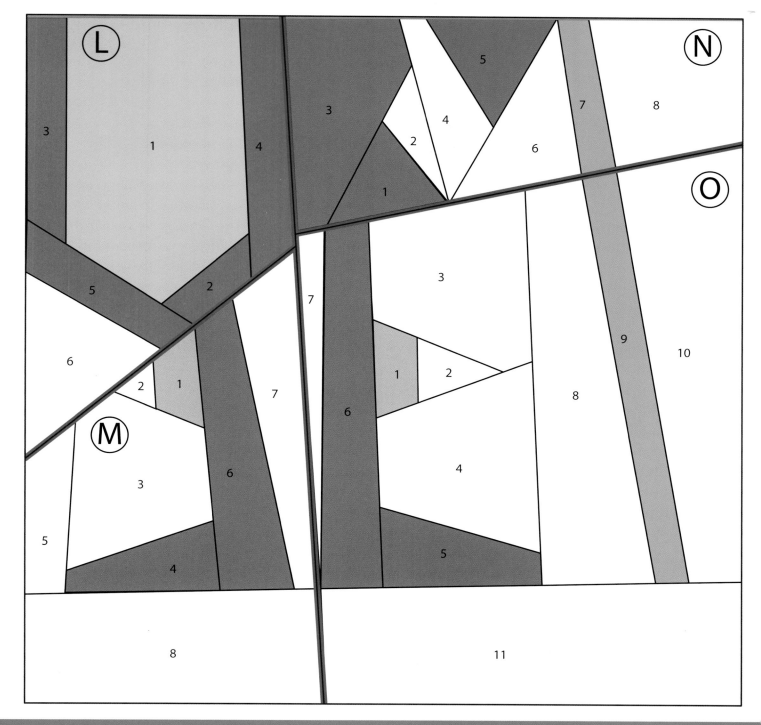

Directions

1. Make 4 copies of the pattern (L, M, N, O).

2. Cut around each segment, adding ¼″ seam allowances.

3. Paper piece each segment.

4. Connect the segments: L to M; N to O; L/M to N/O.

5. Trim ¼″ from the blue line. Match and sew Part 1 to Part 2 on the blue lines.

6. Trim the block to 8″ × 15½″.

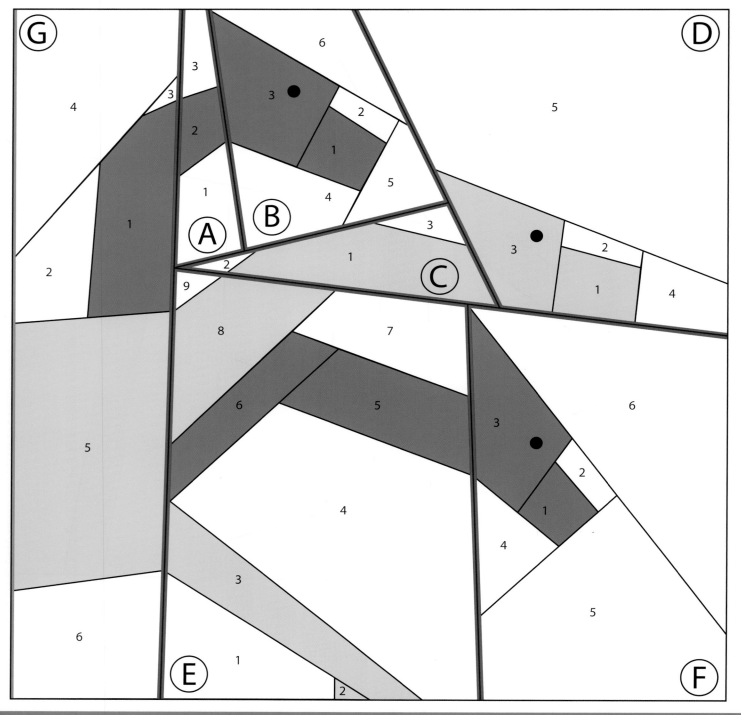

HYDRA, PART 1

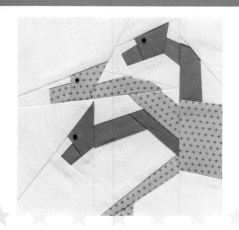

Materials

- 1 fat eighth 9" × 21" of white
- Scraps of light green, dark green, and orange
- Black embroidery floss

Directions

1. Make 4 copies of the pattern (A/D, B/F/G, C, E).

2. Cut around each segment, adding ¼" seam allowances.

3. Paper piece each segment.

4. Connect the segments: A to B to C to D; E to F; A/B/C/D to E/F to G.

5. Trim ¼" from the blue line.

6. Embroider French knots for the eyes.

7. Continue to Hydra, Part 2 (next page).

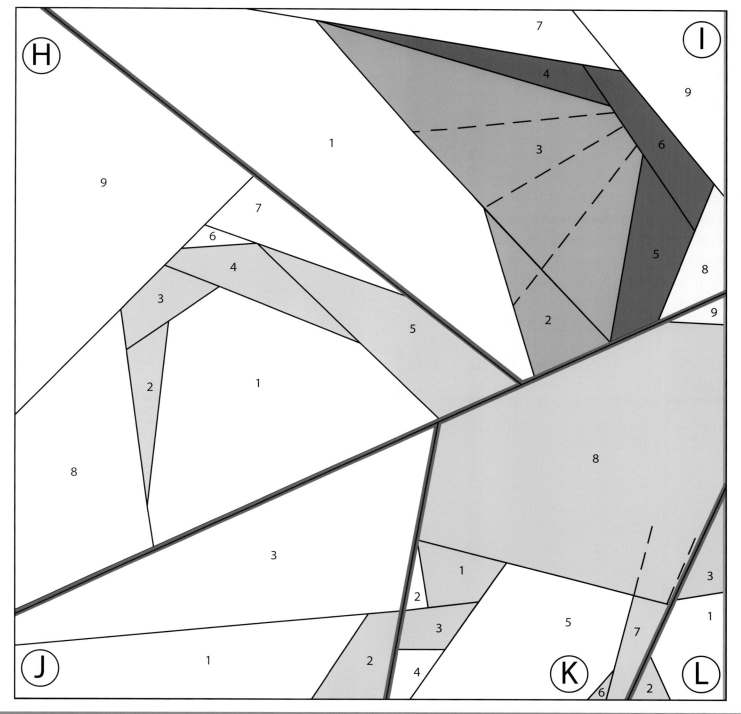

HYDRA, PART 2

Directions

1. Make 3 copies of the pattern (H/L, I/J, K).

2. Cut around each segment, adding ¼″ seam allowances.

3. Paper piece each segment.

4. Connect the segments: H to I; J to K to L; H/I to J/K/L.

5. Trim ¼″ from the blue line. Match and sew Part 1 to Part 2 on the blue lines.

6. Trim the block to 8″ × 15½″.

7. Hand stitch details in the wing and leg.

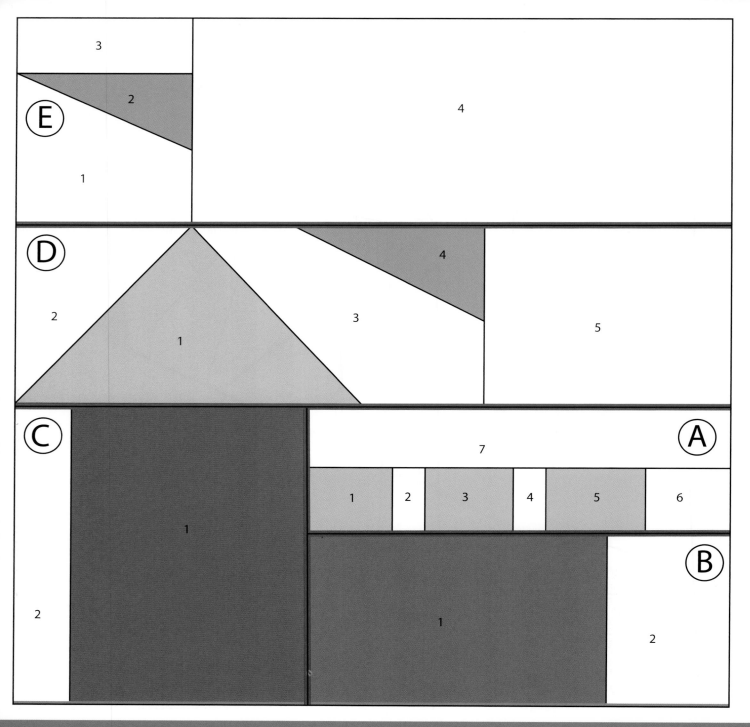

CASTLE, PART 1

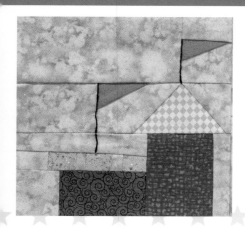

Materials

- 1 fat quarter of light gray
- Scraps of gold, light brown, medium brown, dark brown, brown stripe, medium gray, dark gray, and orange
- Gold metallic and black embroidery floss/thread

Directions

For photo, refer to Castle Blocks Gallery (page 78).

1. Make 3 copies of the pattern (A/E, B/D, C).

2. Cut around each segment, adding ¼″ seam allowances.

3. Paper piece each segment.

4. Connect the segments: A to B to C; D to E; A/B/C to D/E.

5. Trim ¼″ from the blue line.

6. Embroider the flagpoles in black.

7. Continue to Castle, Part 2 (next page).

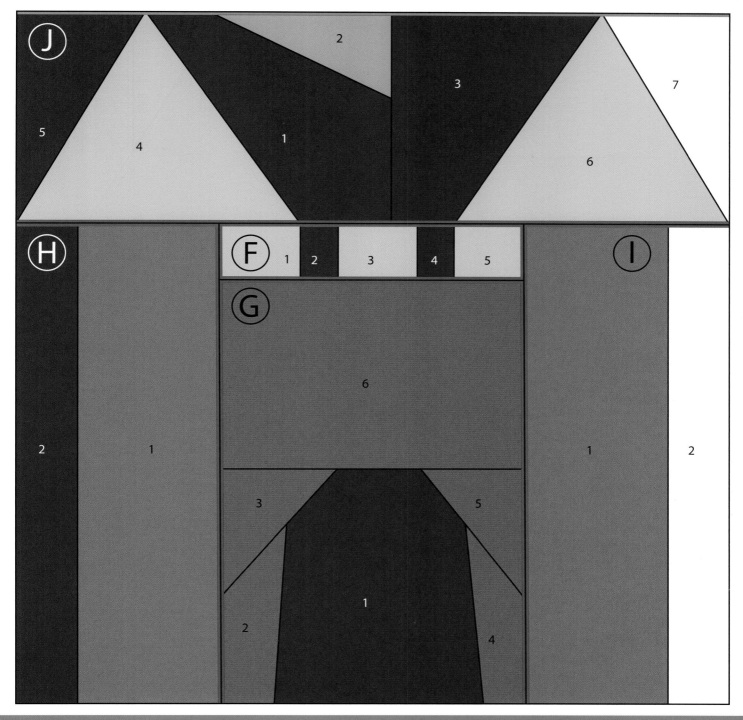

CASTLE, PART 2

Directions

For photo, refer to Castle Blocks Gallery (page 78).

1. Make 3 copies of the pattern (F, G/J, H/I).

2. Cut around each segment, adding ¼″ seam allowances.

3. Paper piece each segment.

4. Connect the segments: F to G to H to I; F/G/H/I to J.

5. Trim ¼″ from the blue line. Match and sew Part 1 to Part 2 on the blue lines.

6. Embroider the flagpole in gold metallic or black (whichever contrasts best with background).

7. Continue to Castle, Part 3 (page 76).

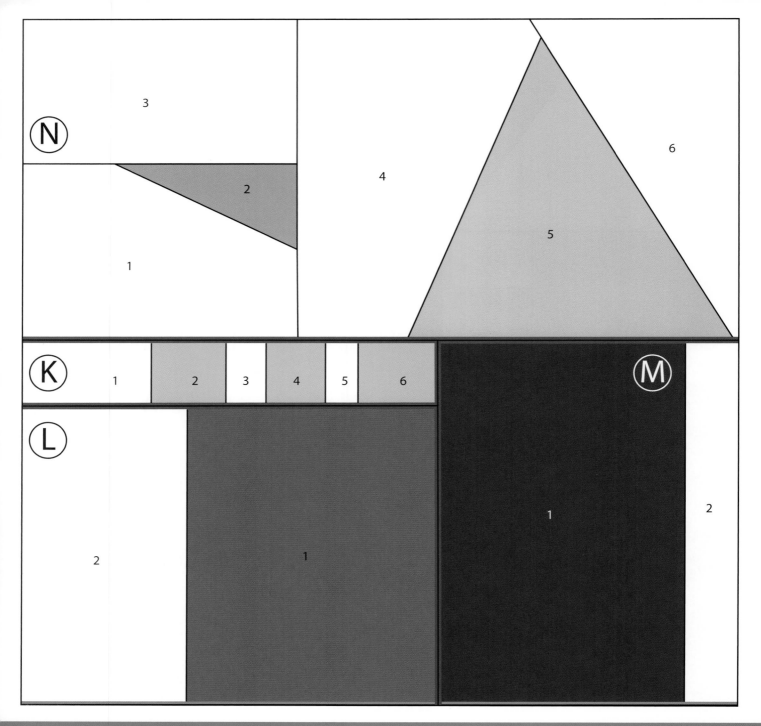

Directions

For photo, refer to Castle Blocks Gallery (page 78).

1. Make 3 copies of the pattern (K, L/N, M).

2. Cut around each segment, adding ¼" seam allowances.

3. Paper piece each segment.

4. Connect the segments: K to L to M; K/L/M to N.

5. Trim ¼" from the blue line.

6. Embroider the flagpole in black.

7. Continue to Castle, Part 4 (next page).

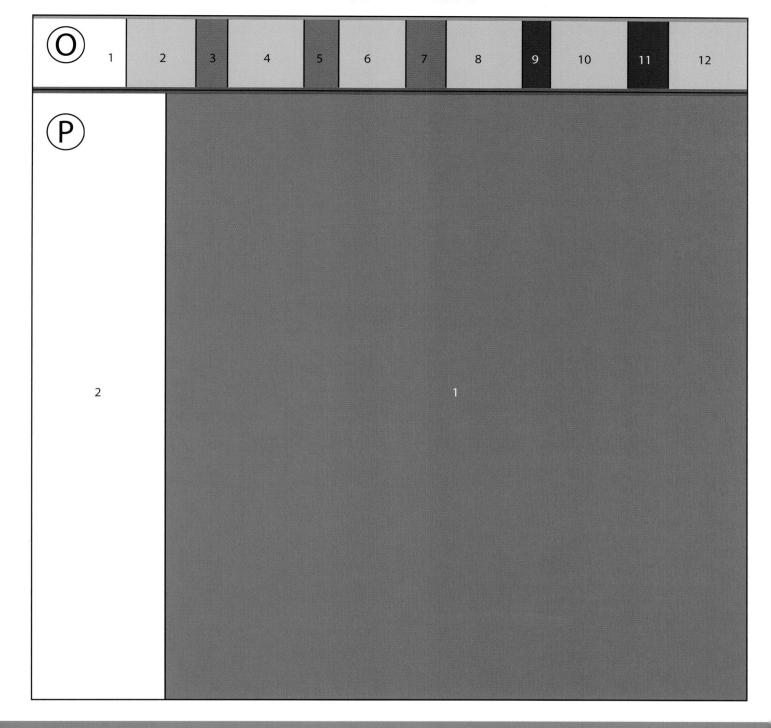

CASTLE, PART 4

Directions

For photo, refer to Castle Blocks Gallery (page 78).

1. Make 2 copies of the pattern (O, P).

2. Cut around each segment, adding ¼″ seam allowances.

3. Paper piece each segment.

4. Connect the segments: O to P.

5. Trim ¼″ from the blue line. Sew Part 3 to Part 4, matching and sewing on the blue lines.

6. Trim the block to 15½″ × 15½″.

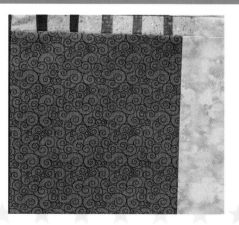

CASTLE BLOCKS GALLERY

Important: *Depending which size Castle block configuration you want to make, note the changes in the background and roof fabrics in the 1- and 2-block variations.*

Castle, using 1 block (Part 2)

Castle, using 4 blocks (Parts 1–4)

GNOME BLOCK FINISHING

Use for Gnome, Part 2 (page 49), Step 7.

Using the Gnome nose pattern (below) and peach fabric, sew a yo-yo. Sew ¼" from the edge of the circle using a running stitch. Pull up the stitches slightly. Add a bit of stuffing. Knot off. Hot glue or hand stitch the nose in place.

Gnome

Nose
3″ circle

Castle, using 2 blocks (Parts 1 and 2)

About the Author

Mary (also known as Marney) Hertel grew up on a small dairy farm in the heart of Wisconsin. Sewing is in her blood, and she likes to say she has "sewn since birth," starting on her mother's sewing machine at a very early age. After securing her art education job straight out of college, she used her first paycheck to purchase a sewing machine. Soon after, she started to quilt and has never stopped.

Mary's favorite method of quilting became paper piecing after she was introduced to this practice in 2013. The puzzle-like quality of paper piecing appealed to Mary and has quickly become her favorite approach to adding an image to a quilt.

Her quirky animal designs are a nod to 35 years of teaching children's art. "I try to keep my animal designs childlike, but expressive," Mary says. She also strives to offer her customers very easy paper-pieced patterns.

Photo by Gail Cameron

Mary has three previously published books, scores of magazine articles, and more than 200 patterns that can be found on Etsy and in many quilting stores throughout the United States.

Enjoy her whimsical designs and her easy-to-paper-piece patterns.

Also by Mary Hertel:

Visit Mary online and follow on social media:

Website: madebymarney.com

Facebook: /madebymarney

Pinterest: /maryhertel

Instagram: @madebymarney

Twitter: @madebymarney

Etsy: etsy.com/shop/madebymarney

Want even more creative content?

Make it, snap it, share it *using #ctpublishing*